YEAR ONE W9-CRI-578

WINTER

An Inspiring Two-Year Journey Through The Bible

Old Testament Devotional Commentary
NIZAR & ELLEN SHAHEEN

New Testament Devotional Commentary
JIM & KATHY CANTELON

Inspirational "Prayer For Today" portions
DAVID & NORMA-JEAN MAINSE

A ministry of Crossroads Christian Communications Inc.

In Canada:
Crossroads Christian
Communications Inc.
100 Huntley Street
Toronto, Ontario
M4Y 2L1

Bus: (416) 961-8001

In the USA:
Crossroads Christian
Communications Inc.
Box 486
Niagara Falls, NY
14302

Prayer: (416) 961-1500

ISBN 0-921702-11-6
Copyright 1989 ©**CROSSROADS CHRISTIAN COMMUNICATIONS INC.**

Published by **CROSSROADS CHRISTIAN COMMUNICATIONS INC.**
100 Huntley Street, Toronto, Ontario, Canada M4Y 2L1

Printed in Canada
Harmony Printing Limited
123 Eastside Drive, Toronto, Ontario, Canada M8Z 5S5

Scripture quotations are from the New King James Version and are used with permission of Thomas Nelson Publishers. Copyright ©1979, 1980, 1982.

Holy Land photos courtesy of the Israel Government Tourist Office, Toronto.

Published Quarterly — second class pending.

"The heavens declare the glory of God; And the firmament shows His handiwork. DAY UNTO DAY utters speech, and night unto night reveals knowledge."
— Psalm 19:1,2

Dear Reader,

The phrase, "Day unto day", found in Psalm 19:2, is most meaningful to us all. Our Old Testament devotional commentary writer for this series, Nizar Shaheen, is fluent in the original language of the Old Testament. He tells me that this Hebrew phrase does not just mean "day to day" or "day after day", but rather means "one day flowing into the next without any break". I'm sure this is the way God wants our relationship with Him to be.

Psalm 19:2 is a very special verse to me personally, because God used the words "Day unto day" to speak to me many years ago about the need for daily Christian television and the importance of hearing from God daily through the reading of His Word.

We've entitled this devotional commentary series *Day Unto Day*, after Psalm 19:2. It is designed to guide you through God's Word in two years while giving you fresh devotional thoughts inspired by each day's reading.

Also, I asked Lorne Shepherd, our 100 Huntley Street Minister to the Family, to write a page about family devotions. Lorne has a phenomenal track record of helping people enrich their family lives.

My prayer for all who read these volumes is that God's glory will be revealed to you "Day unto Day".

In Christ's love and service,

David Mainse
Host of "100 Huntley Street"

Applying this Guide to Family Devotions

by Lorne Shepherd
100 Huntley Street's Minister to the Family

Many families have good relationships but do not feel close to one another spiritually. Spiritual oneness is important. In fact, if a husband and wife regularly read the Bible together, pray together, and attend church, their chances of divorce drops from one in two marriages to one in four hundred. Family devotions are important!

However, sometimes it is hard to make daily prayer times a habit. Here are some practical steps that will help you to have a spiritual unity in your family.

1. Read the Bible passage and devotional comments with your family or spouse.

2. Each member of the family should discuss something they received from the devotional.

3. During your day, find a scripture that will bless your mate or family members. Do not preach at one another with scriptures.

4. Pray for each of your family member's needs.

5. Start off slowly. Do not feel you have to pray for half an hour. Time with God should be enjoyable. Expand your devotional time as your relationship with God grows.

6. If you have children, sing a children's chorus and tell a parallel real life story that will help them understand the devotional guide's lessons. Make it fun!

Special Note for Singles — during your day, find someone with whom you can share the principles God has given you during your devotional study.

Introduction

"Day Unto Day" is a new devotional commentary for the nineties! This book is the first of eight volumes which will lead you on a journey through the entire Bible in two years. It's more than a typical daily devotional, and it does not pretend to be an exhaustive commentary. It is designed to lead us deeper and higher into the knowledge of the Almighty God, and His Son, the Lord Jesus Christ, through the teaching of the Holy Spirit.

The authors, Jim and Kathy Cantelon with the New Testament and Nizar and Ellen Shaheen, the Old Testament, are uniquely qualified for the task. Both have spent many years in the land of the Bible. Let's meet them now:

Jim Cantelon — Jim was the Pioneer Pastor of the Jerusalem Christian Assembly and remained there for seven years. Prior to going to Jerusalem he served successfully as a Canadian Pastor. His practical application of Scripture was well honed as a popular Canadian open-line radio host. In Jerusalem, he continued on radio covering the Middle East regularly, and became deeply involved in the life of the city as a Rotary Club executive. A most unusual congregation of several hundred members was solidly established. His book, "Theology for Non-Theologians" has had excellent reviews in several leading magazines and is published by MacMillan — the fact that this usually "non-religious" publisher would enthusiastically publish his book is a testimony to what is in store for you in your New Testament readings.

Kathy Cantelon — In Jerusalem she was known as Kathy Kennedy for security reasons. Millions knew her through the nightly television news. Her insightful presentation drew a host of loyal viewers. As the daughter of Rev. and Mrs. E. Howard Kerr, and then a Pastor's wife and mother of three, her down-to-earth insights, joined with those of Jim, her husband, are treasured.

Nizar Shaheen — Here is an Arab native of Israel, perfectly fluent in Arabic and Hebrew, the languages of the Middle East and of the Old Testament. His ancestral family home is in the village of Cana of Galilee, not far from Nazareth where he was born. In his teen years, he became a boxer. He trained by running from Cana to the sea of Galilee, a distance of fifteen miles. Upon arrival at the sea, he would plunge in, swim vigorously, and then return home. Following his miraculous conversion, he applied that same tremendous drive to reading and re-reading the Bible many times a year. Before long, he was ministering extensively in the churches of Israel and the West Bank, as well as preaching and teaching in various countries at seminars and conferences. His study of the ancient culture of peoples of the Middle East have given him most enlightening insights on Old Testament passages. He studied theology in Brussels for four years and received his degree in theology. Today, he hosts an Arabic television program called, "Light for All the Nations" which reaches the immigrant population from Arab countries here in the west and also covers many countries through "Middle East Television". He is known by many who hear him as "a teacher's teacher".

Ellen Shaheen — It was during her undergraduate work at "The American Institute of Holy Land Studies", located on Mount Zion in Jerusalem, that she met Nizar; she met him near the end of eight months of concentration on Biblical Hebrew, Archeology, and historical Geography of the Holy Land. Their marriage in Cana of Galilee was a traditional Middle Eastern wedding. During the ceremony, when Ellen spoke in the language of Cana, Arabic, and said the words of Ruth, "Thy people shall be my people and thy God, my God", the crowd cheered and took her to their heart. Into her participation with Nizar in the writing of the Old Testament devotional commentaries, she brings a liberal arts degree with a Biblical Studies major. She also brings her upbringing in a minister's home, that of her parents, David and Norma-Jean Mainse. This mother of three active children has spent many hours studying with her husband in the preparation and writing of this fresh material.

David and Norma-Jean Mainse — It was in 1962, at 25 and 22 years of age, that they began regular Christian television programming. Now this work continues with the daily "100 Huntley Street" telecast, the children's productions and the many non-English programs. From the TV programs have been birthed Circle Square Ranches for youth across the continent and overseas missions in many countries. God has obviously blessed David and Norma-Jean. They have taken each of the commentaries of Jim and Kathy, Nizar and Ellen and have written a "Prayer for today" which you can use as a short starter for your daily prayer time. In these short prayers, they have used the term "we" rather than "I" because they pray together and are thinking of all who will participate with them in the *Day Unto Day* readings.

May this work be a great blessing to you as you grow stronger in the Lord through reading His Word and prayer — DAY UNTO DAY!

Now, your two-year journey begins...

YEAR ONE
JANUARY

*The Jordan River as it flows from Mount Hermon
in Northern Israel.*

Introduction to
The Book of Genesis

Genesis, is a Greek word meaning "origin, source, or beginning". In the original language of Hebrew, the title is *Bereshith*, meaning "in the Beginning". Throughout the whole book, we learn about beginnings. The beginning of the universe, man, sin, family, covenants, promises, government, the Hebrew nation, and most importantly, the beginning of salvation.

Genesis is not a book of history, nor of science, though it contains some of both. It is primarily a book about the history of the redemption of man, therefore it views history with a spiritual perspective. From the creation of mankind, we see the beginning of God's plan of salvation. Genesis clearly expresses the sovereignty of God (in His dealings with the Patriarchs — Abraham, Isaac, Jacob), the justice of God (in punishing sin — the flood, Sodom and Gomorrah), and His grace and mercy toward mankind, which all comes as a result of the love that God has for us, the crown of His creation. We learn of the faithfulness and even the terrible mistakes and sins that the heroes made, however no attempt is made to cover-up or defend their wrongdoings. We see the sinfulness of Adam and Eve, the drunkeness of Noah, the lies of Abraham, Isaac and Rachel, the deceit of Jacob, and the fornication of Judah, yet God in His grace was forgiving and still used them to fulfill His purpose. We can learn from their mistakes, and we can also, in many respects, follow their good examples. This serves to attest to the authenticity, infallibility, and accuracy of the Bible.

Moses, under the inspiration of the Holy Spirit, wrote the first five books of the Bible (the Pentateuch). Jesus Himself attests to the Mosaic authorship (Luke 16:31; 24:44), in fact He says Moses wrote about Him (John 5:46). It is true, Christ is prophesied about several times throughout the book of Genesis and is found in *type* (a historical fact which illustrates a spiritual truth) where Christ is seen in people and events, and Jesus may be seen in the form of *Christophany* (the appearance of the preincarnate Son of God).

The Book of Genesis consists of four main events and four main people. The events: creation, the fall, the flood, and Babel. The people: Abraham, Isaac, Jacob, and Joseph. It is the foundational book for the whole Bible and in it we find, in seed form, many of the great Christian doctrines like redemption and justification by faith. Prayerfully read the Holy Word of God. He will enlighten your understanding and you will be spiritually enriched.

Read Genesis 1 & 2 *January 1*

Key Verse: Genesis 1:27 *"So God created man in His own image..."*

In these first two chapters of the Bible, we come to understand how the world and all that is in it came into being. Our all powerful God created everything there is out of nothing. He merely spoke the word and it was. In fact, all His marvelous creation was found to be *"very good"* (Gen. 1:31).

Mankind was the grande finale, the crown and climax of His creation. Only with the creation of the first man and woman did there proceed a divine counsel and an announcement showing the dignity, high position, and importance of mankind (Gen. 1:26). Although all the animals and birds were formed out of the ground (Gen. 2:9), it was only man into whose nostrils God breathed the breath of life (Gen. 2:7). Thus the human race was made in the image of God. What kind of image was this? Was it a physical likeness? Most certainly not, for God is Spirit and does not have physical parts like a man.

(1) It was a mental likeness. God endowed mankind with the gift of reason, conscience, and will, making him a free agent.

(2) It was a moral likeness. Adam and Eve were made righteous and holy and were therefore able to have communion with God. This moral likeness of sinlessness was lost when Adam and Eve exercised their free will and fell into sin. From then on, mankind suffered the loss of a holy and righteous nature. We are now born with a sinful nature, but through faith in Jesus Christ, we can be renewed to this original likeness of God (Romans 3:21-24; Colossians 3:10; Ephesians 4:23, 24). This is called spiritual regeneration or the process of sanctification.

(3) It was a social likeness. God has a social nature, and He created people to have fellowship with Him. God gave them a social nature as well; consequently, human beings seek for and need fellowship and love. The most fulfilling fellowship is that which we have with God. God loves you and desires that you would love Him and daily commune with Him in prayer.

(4) It was a rulership likeness. Mankind has a similarity to God at least partially fulfilled in his having been created to rule over the earth. Just as God is sovereign over all, man was intended to share in this dominion by God's will.

What an honour it is to be made in the image of God. It should make us desire to bring glory to our Maker. Each human life is very important and worthy of respect. You are important to God and He sent His Son Jesus into the world so that through Him you might be saved, restored, and brought into communion together.

Prayer for today: *Lord, be glorified in our lives. Thank You for salvation, restoration and communion. Change us, Lord, from "glory to glory" until we are conformed to Your image.* (2 Corinthians 3:18)

Read Genesis 3 January 2

Key Verse: Genesis 3:9 *"Then the Lord God called to Adam and said to him, 'Where are you?'."*

Genesis 3 is a very important chapter in the Bible. In it is found the divine explanation of the present fallen condition of mankind. We learn of the subtle devices of our enemy, Satan. We see the effects of sin upon mankind and the environment, and we hear prophesied and promised, for the first time, the gracious provision of salvation which God has made for us.

After Adam and Eve disobeyed God and ate from the forbidden tree of good and evil, the Lord God came walking, as usual, in the garden where He would have fellowship with Adam and Eve. However, this time the condition of Adam and Eve and their response to God was radically changed. Instead of happily receiving the Lord's presence, they hid amongst the bushes. God, who knows all, knew where Adam was hiding, yet He called out to him, *"Where are you?"*. He wanted Adam to come out, stand before Him, and confess his sin openly. God's inquiry was addressed to the condition of man, rather than to his place of hiding.

What condition was this, and what are the results of sin?

(1) The first result of sin we see is **shame**. Adam and Eve recognized that they were naked, not only physically, for their new sinfulness was brought out in plain view (cf. John 3:20).

(2) Sin brings **fear**. They were afraid to approach the Holy God, knowing they had disobeyed Him and that they would now have to be judged.

(3) Sin brings **enmity**. Adam did not protect his wife; rather he blamed her. Their love was not as it was. There was also enmity to the serpent. And sin brings enmity to God, for man and God became separated.

(4) Sin brings **death**. The Bible says, *"the wages of sin is death"* (Romans 6:23). Adam and Eve died a spiritual and moral

death. Their close fellowship with their loving Creator and their innocence was forever gone. Now they were filled with decay and death.

(5) Sin brings **suffering**. Mankind and even the earth was cursed because of Adam's sin. Adam and Eve were expelled from the beautiful garden and now had to work very hard to get the land to produce food. Suffering and difficulties became a usual way of life.

The Lord God, however, did not abandon them. His gracious pursuit showed kindness and mercy. He called out unto Adam to recover and reclaim him. Before God pronounced judgment upon the human race, He pronounced salvation — the messianic promise in Genesis 3:15c that the seed of woman, that is Jesus, will crush the serpent's (Satan's) head. This is evidence of God's love and deep desire to save mankind. The sin of man was not a surprise to God. God had provided redemption even before the foundation of the world. His plan was to save mankind from his sin and suffering. What a great love God has for you!

We no longer need to approach God with fear and shame, rather we can now approach Him with humble boldness if we be clothed and armed with the righteousness of Christ, for nothing but this will cover the shame of our nakedness. Therefore, put on the Lord Jesus Christ and draw near unto God (Revelations 3:18; 2 Corinthians 6:7).

Prayer for today: *Here we are again Lord. We come boldly before Your throne of grace because we are dressed in Christ's righteousness. Thank You for the restoration of fellowship with You. Lead us today in Your perfect will.*

Read Genesis 4 & 5 *January 3*

Key Verse: Genesis 4:7 *"If you do well, will you not be accepted? And if you do not do well, sin lies at the door."*

The murder of Abel by his brother Cain is a tragic account and the direct result of the sinful condition of man due to the Fall. Cain represents all those who try to please God through their own efforts, without total obedience to Him. The Bible seems to imply that God gave Adam and his family instructions on the type of sacrifice which was acceptable and pleasing unto Him. Obedience to the Lord is required in order to be acceptable.

The key verse is a rhetorical question meaning "yes, if you do well (by obeying the Lord), you will indeed be accepted." Cain's offering was given out of a proud, boastful, and disobedient heart and it was from the fruit of the earth, which had been cursed. But Abel's offering was one of blood, and the shed blood of the Old Testament sacrifices was a symbol of the blood that Christ would shed for the remission of sin (see Hebrews 9:22). Along with that, Abel's offering was given from the right kind of heart, one which by faith believes and obeys God. His offering, as Hebrews 11:4 explains, is a witness that he was righteous.

God gave Cain the opportunity to repent and have a second chance; but rather than doing so, his anger and jealousy arose to the point of planning his own brother's murder. Cain did not "do well" and obey God, nor did he heed the Lord's warning; therefore, sin did indeed lie at the door. Full of jealousy, deceit and guile, Cain approached Abel and convinced him to go out to the field with him. Abel, a trusting, honest man was the first victim of such a crime, for there his brother murdered him.

In order to give Cain an opportunity to confess and repent, God asked him for the whereabouts of his brother. Once again he does not repent, but rather expresses the wrong attitude that sadly some believers have today — "Am I my brother's keeper?" God's judgment was considered unbearable by Cain, but God is just and holy, and sin must be punished. The land that Cain loved so much would now no longer yield abundance as it did for him before. Now he would be forced to roam about as a vagabond. He feared that out of vengeance he might be killed and so God put a mark upon him to warn other men not to kill him, for it was not until after the Flood that capital punishment was instituted (see Genesis 9:6).

Cain's descendants proved to be an ungodly lot who were worldly and wicked. But God blessed Adam and Eve with many sons and daughters and one son in particular was given to replace Abel...this was Seth. His descendants were godly and from his line came such men as Enoch who walked with God and was translated by Him, and Methuselah whom God blessed with the longest life, and Noah, the only man in his generation who found favour in the sight of the Lord. God's blessings for the righteous are passed down even to their descendants. If we live obedient, holy and righteous lives, we can have confidence that our families and descendants will also be blessed by God. Of course, the most important blessing is spiritual, that our loved ones, and even those yet unborn, will one day experience the saving grace of the Lord Jesus Christ.

Read Genesis 6 & 7 *January 4*

Key Verse: Genesis 7:5 *"And Noah did according to all that the Lord commanded him."*

Wickedness spread throughout the land as the "Sons of God" took as wives the "daughters of men". The most likely interpretation for this is that the men from the godly line of Seth corrupted themselves by not keeping pure and separate from the sinful and worldly line of Cain, so they were pulled down, which is the usual outcome of association with the sinful. We are taught to remain separated from the sinful things of the world (James 1:27; 4:4). In Genesis 6:2 we read that The "Sons of God" lusted after and married the women because they were beautiful, but this alone should be no criterion for marriage. Great wickedness resulted from these marriages, for from the offspring came giants who ruled with great strength and who led the people into sin and ultimate ruin. The earth was filled with violence and evil. The people continued in their sinful ways, not heeding the warnings of Noah. Jesus likened the end times before His coming to how it was in the days of Noah.

Only Noah remained untainted by the sin of the world, for it is written of him that he "walked with God" (verse 9), as did his forefather Enoch. To walk with God means to be in total agreement and communion with Him. As such, Noah found favour in the eyes of the Lord. All the instructions God gave to him concerning the ark were obeyed exactly and without question. Noah put his faith into action, even though it caused him to be the object of ridicule by those who disbelieved. Building the ark was a tremendous project which took 120 years to accomplish. It's length was that of one and a half football fields, and its height was that of a three storey building. After its completion, a pair (male and female) of unclean animals and seven of all the clean animals came and entered the ark as they were compelled by God. The reason for the seven of the clean animals would be to provide food and to have an extra one to sacrifice unto the Lord.

The ark represents God's holiness and justice. The judgment of God became necessary for their sin was too much for His Holiness to contend with any longer. In His judgments, however, the Lord will never let the righteous perish with the wicked, so He planned a way of escape for Noah and his family. The ark also represents God's mercy and love, not only to Noah but to those who perished as well, for He gave them 120 years of grace to repent before the flood waters began to cover the whole face of the earth. The ark is a symbol of God's free gift of salvation for its doors were open for any who believed to enter and receive protection from the destruction of the world. In the same way, we can receive salvation freely by approaching the cross of the Lord Jesus Christ and thus be secure and hid with Him, protected and covered by His precious blood.

Prayer for today: *Our God and Father, may none of our family be left behind when You close the door of mercy. By Your grace, please bring millions more into Your ark of safety. We praise You for Your righteous judgment.*

Read Genesis 8 & 9   *January 5*

Key Verse: Genesis 8:21 *"And the Lord smelled a soothing aroma. Then the Lord said in His heart, 'I will never again curse the ground for man's sake,...nor will I again destroy every living thing as I have done.'"*

After Noah and his family had been in the ark for 150 days, God, not forgetting His faithful and righteous servant, caused a wind to come over the water which made it begin to recede from the earth, implying the water returned to the seas. God was in control of all that happened and He caused the ark to come to rest on the very high mountains of Ararat (which reach up to 17,000 ft. and are found in present-day Armenia). After the water had totally subsided, God told Noah when it was safe for him and his family and all the living things to leave the ark.

The first thing Noah did was to express his thanks to God by worshipping Him, building an altar and offering unto Him sacrifices from every clean animal and bird. Oral traditions concerning the acceptable offerings may have been passed down to him from his forefathers. We read that the offerings were indeed acceptable, pleasing, and even appeasing unto God, for they came to Him as a "soothing aroma" of satisfaction which caused the Lord God to vow that never again would He destroy the earth as He had done, by a universal flood (8:21; 9:11).

The Lord God blessed Noah and his sons and commanded them to have many children and fill the earth, for they were the starting point of a new human family and history. The old covenant that God established with Adam was not annulled by the Noahian covenant (9:1-19), rather it was reaffirmed and had some additions. The responsibility to populate the earth, man's dominion over the earth, and the covenant as binding on all flesh, were reaffirmed. In addition, man was permitted to eat meat, although not the blood, and the sacredness of human life was established through the institution of capital punishment. The sign of the existence of this everlasting covenant is the rainbow, which also confirms the promise of God that He would never again destroy the whole earth by a flood. The beautiful rainbow also proves to be a message of comfort and love from a just and merciful God.

The story of Noah's drunkedness is sad, for it brought a curse upon his son Ham and all of his descendants. Excessive drinking results in loss of self-control and may even cause one to be mocked and despised by those who are closest relations or friends (see Proverbs 20:1; 23:29-35). Yet, this story reflects the attitude of his children. Ham did not show respect, but the other two brothers took a garment and, without looking upon their father's nakedness, covered him. After Noah arose from his stupor, knowing what had happened he prophetically pronounced a curse and a blessing. **Notice** that he cursed Canaan, the son of Ham to be "servant of servants" which was the lowest, most despised slavery and, in this context, he was foretelling the evil consequences that would befall future generations. Later on, we see that, in God's providence, Ham lived in Canaan and became as wicked as one of them.

This prophecy of Noah was also fulfilled later, when Israel put the Canaanites under subjection (Deut. 7:1,2). Noah pronounced a blessing on Shem by saying "Blessed be the Lord God of Shem" (v.26). Notice also here he did not say "Shem", but "the Lord God of Shem". The more personal name for God, "Jehovah", is used here, for it was through the godly line of Shem that Jehovah Himself, the Lord Jesus Christ, came to the world. Concerning Japheth, Noah said, "May God (here "Elohim") enlarge Japheth, and may he dwell in the tents of Shem", meaning that Japheth (which means "enlarge") will participate in the blessings of Shem, both materially and spiritually.

Let our lives be pleasing to God by following His instructions and let us have the fragrance of Christ, who was that "sweet-smelling", soothing aroma to which all the Old Testament sacrifices pointed (see Ephesians 5:2; 2 Corinthians 2:15).

15

Prayer for today: *Almighty God, we offer the sacrifice of praise — we ask for Your Holy Spirit to make our lives as a delightful perfume of love, joy, righteousness and peace in the midst of the rottenness of this age.*

Read Genesis 10 & 11 *January 6*

Key Verse: Genesis 11:8 *"So the Lord scattered them abroad from there over the face of all the earth, and they ceased building the city."*

After Noah and his family left the ark at the mountains of Ararat, they immigrated about 500 miles to the area of Babylonia. We read in the genealogies of how their families greatly increased, for the Lord God had blessed them. The genealogies of Noah's sons are listed according to their families, languages and nations.

The major races of the world today can be traced to the sons of Noah. The Japhites represent those from the continent of Europe and some of Asia. The Hamites represent those from the continent of Africa who, early in their history, inhabited the land of Canaan. The Shemites represent the Middle Eastern countries, such as Israel and Arabia. Genealogies in the Bible can teach us about ancient history and in the midst of them we often find important pieces of information often overlooked.

From the line of Ham we are told of Nimrod, an important descendant of Cush. He was a mighty hunter, an enthusiastic builder and great leader. He was probably the first king in history. His name means "rebel", for it could very likely have been Nimrod who lead in the rebellious building of the tower of Babel so that his kingdom would remain strong and united. This occurred 100 years after the flood, and still we learn that they did not obey God, for He had commanded the sons of Noah to go and multiply the whole earth (9:1,7); however their descendants had remained together in the same general area of the world.

God was not against civilization, the building of fine structures or cities, or intelligent thinking, but He was against the motivation behind building the tower of Babel, which was a rebellious heart full of self-pride and desiring self-glory, self-honour, and self-rule (sins that God hates the most), all of which put Him out of the picture. The tower was constructed to be a military and municipal building, and some scholars say it may have been a temple built for religious purposes, or for astronomy. Whatever it was for, it was not pleasing to God, so He called a divine council, as He did in Genesis 1:26 before the creation of man, showing the importance of the decision to be made, and it is written, "Let Us" which is in reference to the God-Head — the Holy Trinity.

God's miraculous intervention interrupted and ultimately completely halted the continuation of this great structure. Previous to this, all people spoke the same language and lived in the same general area, but God wanted them to be scattered over the face of the earth, and so this was accomplished by confusing the languages. God has always been involved with the peoples of the world whom He created from "one blood . . . and has determined their preappointed times and the boundaries of their habitation. (Acts 17:26)

Likewise, in the New Testament, Jesus Christ commanded His believers to go into all the world and preach the Gospel (Mark 16:15). However, they continued to congregate at Jerusalem, so God allowed the persecution of the believers which forced them to be scattered throughout the then known world (Acts 8:1), thus the good news spread as God had planned. What happened in the book of Acts is not an accident, we believe it was by divine purpose and the inspiration of the Holy Spirit, that the message reached the three continents which represent the three sons of Noah. For example, the miraculous conversion of the Ethiopian Eunuch, representing Africa and from the line of Ham (Chapter 8), Paul, a Jew from the line of Shem (Chapter 9), and Cornelius, an Italian from the line of Japheth (Chapter 10).

God is no respector of persons, for in Christ there are no differences, we are all one. God's will is that all nations would come unto repentance and worship Him. In the book of Revelations, we are given a wonderful picture of how it will be in heaven when people from every tongue and every nation will be with the Lord, singing His praises (see Rev. 5:9,10). In contrast, later on in the book of Revelation (chapter 18), we see God's judgment on the great Babylonian city which, if we study carefully, we see sins as those who built the tower of Babel, that of being self-centered by unifying nations to lead them astray against God.

Prayer for today: *O God, You are above all and yet You are in our midst. We bow in worship. Grant today that we may tell someone about Your love and that we may help send others to do the same.*

Read Genesis 12 & 13 *January 7*

Key Verse: Genesis 12:1 *"Now the Lord had said to Abram, 'Get out of your country from your kindred, and from your father's house to a land that I will show you.'"*

Here we come to a new era or historical period — God's dealing with a certain man, Abram, later renamed "Abraham", in order to see His divine plan for mankind in progress. God took a special interest in Abram, since he was the "genesis" of the promised seed. Abram was called by God to a life of separation and consecration. He was called to leave his native land, Ur of the Chaldeasis, which was full of idolatry, and headed for an unknown destination. It seems at first he only partially obeyed God's call, for he stopped short of Canaan and lived with his father Terah's household at Haran. After Terah died, God renewed his call to Abram. This meant even further separation, for he was to leave his relatives and his father's household.

Along with this call came several promises: (1) Abundance, "I will make you a great nation." God would do even more than just restore to him that which he had left behind in Haran. (2) Blessing, "I will bless you." This blessing is both spiritual and material. (3) Fame, "[I will make] your name great." Even today in all parts of the world, Abraham's name is well known, honoured and revered. (4) Goodness, "You shall be a blessing." Abram was a friend of God and having constant fellowship with God results in godliness. So Abram affected those who knew him. His very countenance was a witness. (5) Divine justice, "I will bless those who bless you and I will curse him who curses you." Abram wholeheartedly took on God's cause and so here God promises to interest Himself in his. (6) Divine grace. "In you all the families of the earth shall be blessed." This is the greatest promise, for through the seed of Abram came the promised Messiah, Jesus Christ.

All nationalities can enter into the blessings of the Lord through Jesus Christ. He is the greatest blessing ever given to the world.

Abram went forth equipped with the divine promises of God and with faith, knowing that God would guide and protect him. Wherever he travelled and set up his tents, he would build an altar and lead his family in worship of Jehovah. When famine struck the land, however, Abram had a lack of faith, for he travelled to Egypt to live without being instructed by God to do so. While there, because of fear, he lied about his wife. He didn't trust God and hold His promises. Even though we are sometimes unfaithful to Him, God remains faithful as He did with Abram. He delivered Sarah, and thus protected her purity. And He blessed Abram materially in Egypt and when they left, they did so with an abundance. Abram and his household returned to Bethel where he started from and where he had built an altar, and there he "called on the name of the Lord" (Genesis 13:4).

Surely Abram repented for his unfaithfulness and renewed his commitment to the Lord. Likewise, we must return to our first love, learn from our mistakes, and recommit ourselves to God and faithfulness to Him. Abram and his nephew Lot, who was like an adopted son to him, were both blessed materially. So much so, that they had to separate because their combined livestock was over-crowding the available land and thus creating strife. Abram was an honorable and peace-loving man, who even laid aside his right by allowing Lot to choose the land he wanted first. Lot chose the best for himself: the fertile Jordan plain. Abram was content, however, and God blessed him, once again reassuring him that the land around him was his and that his descendants would be too numerous to count. Abram responded in worship to the Lord by building an altar to the Lord in Hebron.

Our future is safe and will be blessed if we, like Abram, seek peace, separate ourselves from sin, and go forth, faithfully worshipping the Lord wherever we are and trusting Him to lead us.

Prayer for today: *Lord, we do worship You today and we are trusting You to lead us. Thank You that You care about the details of our lives.*

Read Genesis 14 & 15   January 8

Key Verse: Genesis 15:6 *"And He believed in the Lord, and He accounted it to Him for righteousness."*

We discover here that not only is Abram a man of peace, but also, when necessary, a man of war who will courageously face the enemy. He loved his nephew Lot, so as soon as he heard of his captivity, he gathered his trained servants and planned the rescue mission. Amazingly, or shall we say, providentially, this risky mission was successful. He caught the enemy at night by surprise and recovered all the goods that had been taken, along with Lot and his household. On their return home, they were met by Melchizedek, king of Salem, the priest of the most high God, who blessed Abram and blessed God for giving Abram the victory. Abram gave him a tithe of all the goods recovered. Melchizedek is referred to by the writer of Hebrews who says Christ is "a priest forever according to the order of Melchizedek" (Hebrews 7:17). Melchizedek was a picture or a type of Christ. We see this in his name, meaning "king of righteousness"; in his position as "king of Salem", meaning "king of peace"; in his title of geneology, "having neither beginning of days nor end of life" (Hebrews 7:3).

The king of Sodom also came out to meet Abram and offered him gifts, but Abram refused so that he would not be obliged to the king of Sodom, nor let him say, "I have made him rich." All the glory for Abraham's riches and indeed all that we have as well, is to God. In chapter 15, we see the covenant of God with Abram. God once again promises Abram that he would have a son of his own. The Lord came to him in a vision, saying, "Do not be afraid." Abram must have been in fear that he would die without a son of his own, for he and his wife were getting old. In his culture, to be without a son was a disgrace and a shame. However, Abram believed God would do as He said and give him a son and numerous descendants. Because of such great faith, the Lord "accounted it to him for righteousness" (Genesis 15:6).

It is wonderful to find these great doctrines of imputed righteousness and justification by faith alone in the beginning of the Bible. In fact, this very verse is quoted four times in the New Testament (Romans 4:3, 22; Galatians 3:6; James 2:23) to show that we can never, on our own merit or good works, attain salvation. It is only through faith and trust in God that we are justified, and only through the vicarious death of Jesus Christ on the cross are we declared righteous.

After Abram offered unto the Lord the prescribed sacrifice, God told him in a dream the reason for the delay in possessing the land — his descendants would be in servitude for about four hundred years in a strange land but would come out with great possessions (Genesis 15:13,14), and that the iniquity of the Amorites is not yet complete (Genesis 15;13). God does not destroy one nation to provide a home for another, even if the other nation be His chosen people. The reason for God's judgment of destruction upon a nation is for punishment only when the iniquity and wickedness has reached an unbearable height (eg. Sodom and Gomorrah, Genesis 19:1-38).

Finally, in chapter 15, God reassures Abram of the great Promised Land his descendants will inherit, the literal borders of which were fulfilled during the reign of Solomon. Amazingly, however, we see in Hebrews 11;10 and 16, that the ultimate Promised Land for the seed of Abram, which is now those who believe in Jesus Christ, is the "heavenly country" (Hebrews 11:16), "the city which has foundations whose builder and maker is God" (Hebrews 11:10). This promise of a heavenly inheritance is for us, as well, who look to Jesus, the author and finisher of our faith.

Prayer for today: *Thank You, Father, for Your Son Jesus. Today and forever we crown Him King of our lives. Reign in righteousness and peace, Lord Jesus.*

Key Verse: Genesis 17:1 *"When Abram was ninety-nine years old, the Lord appeared to Abram and said to him, 'I am Almighty God; walk before Me and be blameless'."*

Abram had been living in the land for ten years already and still did not have the son God had promised him. He and his wife were getting older and becoming discouraged. Rather than waiting for the perfect timing of the Lord, they took the matter upon themselves and jumped ahead, leading to many troubles and strife. Out of desperation, Abram heeded the voice of his wife Sarai to follow the common heathen custom and lie with her maidservant so that she might bear a child for her. He took heed to the wrong voice, for this was not what God had told him to do, nor was it His plan. The promised seed was to come from Abram's wife Sarai. Great strife arose when the maidservant Hagar conceived, for she forgot her position and came to despise Sarai. Abram was in a tight situation, for Sarai complained and put the blame on him. In order to keep the peace, the only solution was to let Sarai have her way and do with Hagar what she wanted.

In those days, in the laws of the land, a servant had no rights. Hagar was forced to flee ('Hagar' means 'to escape' or 'leave') from the harshness of her mistress, but God did not abandon her. For the first time in the Bible we see the appearance of the Angel of the Lord who speaks and comforts Hagar as though he were the Lord Himself. She is told to return and submit to her mistress, then he prophesied that she would have many descendants and prophesied concerning the child within her womb whom he says is to be called Ishmael meaning "God has heard". Hagar was encouraged and proclaimed that God lives and sees.

Thirteen years after Ishmael was born, the Lord once again appeared to Abram in a new revelation of Himself — "I am Almighty God", "El Shadai", expressing God's greatness and omnipotence (all-powerful). Abram needed to be reassured that nothing was impossible for God and to be exhorted to walk blameless before Him. Before God instituted the rite of circumcision, which was to be a covenant sign that they were set apart for Him, God changed Abram's name, meaning "exalted father" to "Abraham" meaning "father of a multitude", for through his promised seed all nations of the earth would be spiritually blessed. Sarai's name was also changed to Sarah (meaning "princess"), and Abraham was told that from her would come the child of promise. Abraham cried out, concerning Ishmael, requesting that he would be blessed. God heard his cry and promised to bless Ishmael and make his descendants many. The Lord's covenant would be established with Isaac, the son Abraham and Sarah were to have one year later. In renewal of the covenant, Ishmael at the age of 13, and Abraham at the age of 99, along with all the other males of his household were circumcised as God commanded.

The exhortation that God gave to Abraham is one we should take for ourselves. Let us walk blamelessly before the Lord.

Prayer for today: *O God we praise You for Your promises and for Your perfect timing in their fulfillment. Grant us Your grace that we may walk blameless before You and before the world.*

Read Genesis 18 & 19 *January 10*

Key Verse: Genesis 18:27 *"Then Abraham answered and said, 'Indeed now, I who am but dust and ashes have taken it upon myself to speak to the Lord'."*

How excited Abraham was to offer hospitality and welcome into his tent three visitors from the Lord. As soon as he saw them, he knew they were no ordinary men, so he ran out and prostrated himself before them and addressed one of them as 'his Lord'. Once again, the Lord reassured Abraham of the son he and Sarah would have. The tent was normally divided into two, as in some Bedouin tents today; one which was open for guests and another was closed and more private. Sarah was likely inside the more private half of the tent listening to their conversation. Sarah laughed in disbelief when she heard them announce that she would have a son, for she was far past the age of bearing a child, and then she lied, denying that she had laughed. She was rebuked for it and told that nothing is impossible for the Lord.

We also see here the amazing friendship between Abraham and the Lord who said, "Shall I hide from Abraham what I am doing...For I have known him" (meaning for a long time they have been close friends)". When God shared His plans with Abraham concerning Sodom and Gomorrah, we see the great love and compassion that Abraham had for the sinful souls in those cities. He interceded on their behalf. Knowing the moral attributes of God, Abraham knew He would never let the righteous perish with the wicked, so he bargained with God to spare the cities if there be just 10 righteous among them. The two angels went to Sodom and found Lot sitting at the gate, meaning he was probably involved in politics and in the leadership of Sodom. Knowing the evil of the city, Lot insisted that the angels enter into his house and stay for the night. At night the men of the city, both young and old, perverted and full of lust came to Lot's house to force him to give them the strangers that they might sexually abuse them. The blatant, open wickedness was more than our Holy God could bear. Destruction was the only fitting judgment for them.

The angels rushed Lot, his wife and two daughters out of the city to flee for their lives. Several things revealed the carnality of Lot, who represents the carnal, compromising believer, whereas Abraham represents the godly, spiritual believer. Lot was living in an evil place and keeping company with sinful, worldly people. This can have a bad effect on those trying to follow the Lord. Lot's problem was that he remained silent and did not try to influence his community to walk in the ways of the Lord, thus he was living in the wrong place (see 2 Peter 2:6-8). He did the wrong thing in offering his two virgin daughters to the wicked men: he had been influenced by the wickedness of the society. He even allowed his other daughters to marry men of Sodom who did not do what was right, for they disrespectfully ignored his warning to them. Then, his insistence to flee to the small city of Zoar, rather than to the mountain where the angel advised him to go, shows he was worldly-minded. Ironically, the mountain is where Lot ended up because he was afraid to live in the city of Zoar.

As well, Lot's wife was caught up with the lifestyle of Sodom and, although she followed the angel and fled, her heart remained there, so when she looked back with longing she became a pillar of salt. Jesus reminded us of this sad incident in Luke 17:32. The wicked lifestyle in the city of Sodom affected his daughters as well, for they committed an awful sin in getting their father drunk so as to conceive children from him. Their descendants of those offspring were the Moabites and the Amonites who became constant enemies of the children of Israel. Lot's compromising and carnal life led to the destruction of his family and all he had worked for in Sodom. His high position and prosperity were in vain, for he lost everything.

We should be as Abraham, thinking spiritually and living humbly before God, rather than as Lot. Jesus likened the days before His coming to how it was in the time of Sodom and Gomorrah, when their wickedness reached heaven. We are living in a similar day such as that, filled with blatant sin. **May the Lord help us not to be conformed to this world and to not compromise with the world**. Although we live in the world, we are not to love and participate in the ungodliness of the world, but if we do the will of God we will abide forever (1 John 2 :15-17).

Prayer for today: *Lord, help us not to be conformed to this world and not to compromise with the world. Praise You for Your gift of overcoming power. By faith we experience Your strength to overcome.*

Read Genesis 20 & 21   *January 11*

Key Verse: Genesis 21:1 *"And the Lord visited Sarah as he had said, and the Lord did for Sarah as He had spoken."*

Abraham traveled south and sojourned in Gerar, a Philistine city about 40 miles west of Hebron, near the coast of the Mediterranean sea. We are not given the reason for his move, but it may have been to find better pastures for his great flocks of livestock to graze.

Once again, Abraham goes through the same kind of experience as he did when he went to Egypt (Gen. 12:10-20). He had not learned his lesson, and so he repeated the same lie that Sarah was his sister. Later he explained to the king that she was his half sister, daughter of his father, but not a daughter of his mother. However, this is no excuse: a half truth is still a lie. In those days it was allowed to marry a half sister, but later on it was forbidden (Lev. 18:9, 20:17, Deut. 27:22). Again, Abraham feared that they would kill him in order to take his beautiful wife. Sarah must have been extremely beautiful for even in her old age she attracted kings and they desired her. God, however, once again protected her purity by warning King Abimelech in a dream. He was so afraid of the consequences of committing such a sin that he arose early to obey the instructions the Lord had given him. With wisdom and calmness, he rebuked Abraham and yet still showed him respect as a prophet of God. Abraham had been the cause of the trouble and so he prayed that God would heal the closed wombs of the women in Abimelech's household and God answered his prayer. Again, the situation turned out for Abraham's good, for the king gave him livestock, servants, and silver along with the permission to dwell anywhere he pleased on the king's land.

God is always faithful, and what He promises we can be confident He will do. Sarah and Abraham, although in their old age, did indeed have the child of promise. God's faithfulness was clearly manifested in the arrival of that long awaited day. The real heir from the free woman was born when Abraham was 100 and Sarah was 90. What a miracle! Nothing is impossible with God. They obeyed the Lord, naming him "Isaac" which means "laughter", for they were both filled with great joy.

Ishmael, however, was filled with jealousy, even to the point of mocking Isaac and, as the Apostle Paul says, "persecuting" him. In Galatians 4:21-31 Paul has drawn an interesting allegory about these two sons of Abraham. The one "born according to the flesh", Ishmael, represents the Mosaic covenant, but the one "born according to the Spirit" represents the covenant of grace which is for Christians, who are children of the promise. "We are not the children of the bondwoman (representing the Old Testament Law) but of the free" (Gal. 4:31).

Abraham, a loving father, was grieved to hear Sarah's request that Ishmael, now 14 years old, and his mother Hagar be cast out. God, however, showed this to be His will, so Abraham yielded to her wishes. This was necessary for the establishment of Isaac in the rights and privileges of the covenant.

For the second time, God graciously heard Hagar's distress and sent an angel to comfort her. Even though Hagar was not from the people of the covenant, He still took care of her and her son Ishmael, whom He had promised to bless.

When God makes a promise, we can be confident that He will accomplish it, and we can trust Him to visit us in our time of need. "By faith Sarah herself also received strength to conceive seed, and she bore a child when she was past the age, because she judged Him faithful who had promised" (Hebrews 11:11).

Prayer for today: *Lord God, as You heard the boy Ishmael and the weeping of his mother, even so we come to You now for deliverance from all those things that would destroy us. Thank You for Your compassion.*

Read Genesis 22 & 23   *January 12*

Key Verse: Genesis 22:12 *"And He said, 'Do not lay your hand on the lad, or do anything to him; for now I know that you fear God, since you have not withheld your son, your only son, from Me'."*

Abraham proved faithful in this most difficult test of obedience: would he be willing to obey God even if it meant sacrificing his long-awaited, precious son? This was a heathen practice, done to appease the gods or find favour with them, yet Abraham was certain he had heard the voice of the one true living God, so without questioning he did as the Lord instructed him. Whom did he love more... God or the son God had promised him?

Abraham was willing to sacrifice his son, believing and trusting that "God was able to raise him up, even from the dead" (Hebrews

11:19). He took Isaac up to Mount Moriah (known today as the Temple Mount in Jerusalem). Believing God would do a miracle, he said to his servants who were waiting for him, "**we** will come back to you" (22:5). It must have broken Abraham's heart when young Isaac asked, "My father...look, the fire and the wood, but where is the lamb for a burnt offering?" (22:7). His reply was prophetic as he told his son that God would provide, and indeed God did provide a ram. Here we have a new revelation of God as "Jehovah Jireh", which means, "the Lord will provide". Because Abraham had proven his obedience, God confirmed the promise that through Abraham's seed the whole world would be blessed (i.e. through Jesus Christ) and the covenant between them was reaffirmed.

Those who faithfully stand in a time of testing will come out of it pure as gold; all others will be burned like hay and wood (1 Corinthians 3:11-15; 1 Peter 1:7). God expects that those whom He calls to a position of leadership will stand firm under testings and trials. He never tempts us with evil (James 1:13), but God tests the righteous as He did with Abraham (Psalm 11:5; James 1:3).

Abraham grieved at the great loss of his wife, Sarah, who died at age 127, and for the first time he considered buying land so that he might have a suitable burial place for her. It is amazing that Abraham; although very rich, never owned any land until this time. God had promised all this land would be for him and his descendants, so he was waiting patiently for this to be accomplished, all in God's perfect timing.

Because Abraham was an honourable, humble man, the people showed tremendous respect and called him "a mighty prince among them" (23:6). He purchased the field of Machpelah beside Hebron and buried Sarah in the cave which was on that land. Later, Abraham himself was buried in that cave, as were his descendants, Isaac and Jacob, as well as Rebekah and Leah.

Prayer for today: *O God, Your Word tells me that "the fear of the Lord is the beginning of wisdom." Grant that we may have the wisdom that comes from our reverent fear of You and may it result in obedience to You.*

Read Genesis 24 *January 13*

Key Verse: Genesis 24:12 *"Then he said, 'Oh Lord God of my master Abraham, please give me success this day, and show kindness to my master Abraham'."*

This most beautiful story expresses the goodness and guidance of God. Abraham, at 140 years of age, possibly thought he was close to death, thus he wanted to settle important matters before he died. In order to keep his descendants in the godly line of Shem and to remain separate from the sinful idolatry of Canaan, he felt it necessary that his son Isaac (now 40 years old) marry a girl from his own family (Nahor or Haran in Mesopotamia) rather than a Canaanite woman. Abraham told his servant that Isaac was not to go; he was to stay in the land God had promised them while a servant would search for a wife. He made his oldest servant, probably Eliezer of Damascus (cf. chapter 15:2), take a solemn vow by putting his hand under Abraham's thigh. In this ancient custom, the thigh symbolized the organs of procreation and an oath made in this manner was particularly sacred and binding.

Abraham's loyal servant was wise and God-fearing — a great example of faithfulness, obedience, and trust. His obligation to find a wife for Isaac took him quite a distance away and the angel of the Lord went before him (24:7). He knew how to pray and worship God (24:12;26) and believed God would answer Abraham's prayers and his. The servant prayed God would grant him success in his mission and would show "kindness" (i.e. "hesed" in the Hebrew, meaning grace and favour) to his master Abraham. Even before he had finished praying, God began to answer his specific prayers, for along came Rebekah, the daughter of Abraham's brother's son, (which made her Isaac's second cousin). In those days, the young women would go as a group to draw water from the well at dawn and at dusk. Rebekah, a beautiful young lady, was among those who came at dusk to fill their water jugs. She did exactly as the servant had prayed, and it was no small task to draw plenty of water for ten thirsty camels. When Abraham's servant spoke with her family, he was totally honest and gave glory to God. It seems Rebekah had a godly family and her father Bethuel and brother Laban discerned this was of the Lord (24:50,51).

The servant, excited at the success of his mission and anxious to return, wanted to depart with Rebekah the next morning. She and her family agreed. Upon seeing Isaac, Rebekah dismounted from her camel showing respect, then she veiled her face, since it was the Eastern custom that the groom not see the bride without her face veiled until after their marriage.

God clearly was the One who had chosen Isaac's mate for him and God used the servant to accomplish His plan. The union was successful, for we are told Isaac loved her (24:67). In today's western society, it is unthinkable for another to choose one's mate for it is a personal decision between the two who want to wed. In Isaac's case, it was with God's guidance and prayer that his spouse was chosen, and this is the right principle for us today as well. **In fact, in all important decisions we should pray for God's guidance and His will, and trust Him, for He is faithful.**

Prayer for today: O Lord, we pray that You will guide us in our decisions today and every day.

Read Genesis 25 & 26   January 14

Key Verse: Genesis 26:28 *"But they said, 'We have certainly seen that the Lord is with you'...*

Abraham married Katurah after Sarah's death, and even though his body was considered "dead" since he was 100 (Romans 4:19; Genesis 17:17), he was blessed by the Lord with six more sons. However, Isaac remained his sole heir since God had established His covenant with him, and through him would come the promised Seed (Jesus Christ) that would bless all the earth (Genesis 17:19; 26:4; Galatians 3:8). To his other children Abraham gave gifts and sent them eastward so that the territory of Canaan would remain for Isaac. The descendants of those other sons became the Midianites. Ishmael, Abraham's son from the maidservant Hagar, lived to the southeast of Canaan in the large territory called the Arabian Peninsula. The Lord blessed Ishmael with 12 sons, as the prophecy had foretold, and they did, in fact become a great nation (Genesis 17:20).

Abraham, the greatest and most venerated of the patriarchs, lived a long, successful life, pleasing unto the Lord. At the age of 175, this "friend of God" and "father of the faithful" went on to an even closer fellowship with the Lord in glory. Ishmael must haved loved his father dearly, for he, along with Isaac, returned to bury him. Thirty-eight years after Sarah's death, Abraham was buried beside her in the cave of Machpelah.

God's blessing was passed down from Abraham to Isaac, who greatly increased in wealth. However, his wife Rebekah was barren and unable to bear children for 20 years, but God heard Isaac's desperate prayers and she became pregnant. After she conceived, God foretold that these twins would be two different nations and the elder would serve the younger (25:23). A fulfillment of this prophecy is seen when King David, Jacob's descendant, subjected the Edomites, Esau's descendants (2 Samuel 8:14). The Apostle Paul speaks of God's predestination on the basis of foreknowledge and illustrates it with the prophecy about Jacob and Esau (Romans 9:10-13).

Esau, the firstborn, was entitled to the "birthright", which meant he would receive a double portion of his father's inheritance. However, in the patriarchal line, this included the spiritual blessing and privilege of carrying on the Messianic lineage as well. We are told Esau cared nothing for his birthright. He was ungodly and not interested in its significance, so he took an oath and sold it for a bowl of lentil stew (cf. Hebrews 12:16, 17).

Twice in chapter 26 the Lord confirms the same promise of blessing that He had made to Abraham. An example of God's blessing is that, during the famine, He told Isaac **not** to go to Egypt. Because of his obedience, God blessed him and during that year he sowed and reaped a hundredfold (26:12), which made the Philistines in the land very jealous. They caused him much trouble concerning his wells, yet rather than fighting and quarreling, Isaac proved to be peace-loving and graciously moved on until he dug a well that was not disputed. Abimelech, king of the Philistines, must have feared Isaac since he was mightier than they and sent him away from their territory (26:16). Later, upon clearly seeing that the Lord God was with him, Abimelech journeyed to meet Isaac and made a treaty with him, wanting to befriend him. This was wise, for as the promise was to Abraham, so it was to Isaac, "I will bless those who bless you. . . curse him who curses you" (12:3). The Lord honours those who honour Him and this is evidenced in the life of Isaac.

Prayer for today: *Father God, we honour You for who You are. Help us to live in such a way that the people around us will honour You also.*

Read Genesis 27   January 15

Key Verse: Genesis 27:33 *"Then Isaac trembled exceedingly and said, '. . . I have blessed him — and indeed he shall be blessed'."*

Although Isaac was a peaceful man, at times there was great lack of peace within his home because of the favouritism he and Rebekah showed their sons. Isaac loved Esau who was a strong, masculine-looking hunter, but Rebekah loved Jacob, a mild-mannered homebody (25:27,28). Another cause of unrest within the home was that Esau, still unconcerned for spiritual things, had married two local Hittite women, thus grieving his parents (26:34,35), for the Hittites were idolotrous pagans.

The birthright and the blessing are two separate things, but they go hand in hand. Jacob had cunningly taken away from Isaac the birthright, which primarily emphasized the physical inheritance, but the blessing emphasized both physical and spiritual blessing. Esau, as the older of the twins, was entitled to both the birthright and the blessing, but God had a different plan and purpose. Even before their birth, He foresaw their hearts and chose Jacob (25:23).

Isaac wanted to give the blessing to Esau before he died, but Rebekah, overhearing and knowing Jacob earnestly desired it (which was God's channel of blessing to the whole world), conspired with him to deceive Isaac, now old and blind. Their scheme worked. The way they went about it was wrong, and certainly God could have accomplished it in another and better way, but He permitted it to happen so that Isaac would give Jacob the blessing instead of Esau. We see, however, that Jacob (whose name means "deceiver") later on in life paid much for his deception and lies. Isaac should have known from the prophecy (25:23), and from the fact that Esau married outside of the godly line, that Esau could never carry on the promised blessing of the Lord. Maybe Isaac's love for Esau blinded him from seeing the truth.

The blessing of the patriarchs could not be annulled or changed; that is why Isaac could not change the blessing he had just given to Jacob, even though he desperately wanted to. Esau finally realized what he had despised and now had lost, so he wept and pleaded with his father to bless him also, but what more was there to say? The writer of the book of Hebrews uses this as an illustration, saying because Esau was profane and "found no place for repentance", he was rejected (Hebrews 12:16,17). Isaac prophesied that although he (i.e. his descendants, the Edomites) would serve his brother, there would come a time when he would throw off his yoke (Israel, Jacob's descendants — see 2 Kings 8:20-22).

Esau's anger turned to hate for his brother (27:41) and bitterness so filled his heart that he decided to kill Jacob as soon as their father died. Isaac, however, was not as close to death as he or Esau thought, for he lived about 80 more years after blessing Jacob. It seems God made Isaac well after the blessing was given to the right person. Isaac saw that the will of God was accomplished, even though initially he had been stubborn and tried to stop it.

The plan and purpose of our all-knowing, infinite God is sometimes beyond our finite understanding. If it were according to deeds that Jacob and Esau had done, they would both be rejected. The same would go for us too (Ephesians 2:8,9; Titus 3:5; Romans 9:10-16). But God does what He pleases and knows what He is doing. His choosing is built on His eternal plan, moral attributes, and character. In His grace and by His will, He has predestined our salvation before the foundation of the world. He has called us His children and heirs, and there is a divine purpose in our calling (Epesians 1:5,11). Let us gives thanks to the Lord for His grace. **Let us live out faithfully the calling that God has for us.**

Prayer for today: *Lord, thank You for Your grace in calling me, and help me to live faithfully the calling and purpose You have for my life.*

Read Genesis 28 & 29   *January 16*

Key Verse: Genesis 28:2 *"Arise, go to Padan Aram, to the house of Bethuel your mother's father; and take yourself a wife from there...".*

Isaac reaffirmed to Jacob the blessing of Abraham, and,like his father Abraham (24:3), Isaac told his son to not take a wife from the daughters of Canaan, but to return to their relatives, to the household of Rebekah's brother Laban, in order to marry a godly wife. Jacob obeyed his father's instructions and left for Padan Aram, which was where his mother had already told him to go out of fear that Esau would kill him. Esau heard his father instructing Jacob not to take a wife from the Canaanites and finally realized the grief his Canaanite wives had caused his father, so he tried to please him and show respect by marrying a relative as well (28:8,9). He married his uncle Ishmael's daughter who would have learned about the God of Abraham. Possibly Esau had learned his lesson (although the hard way) and had begun to consider spiritual things more seriously.

On Jacob's journey, an unusual thing happened at Luz, which he renamed "Bethel", meaning "house of God". The ladder, with angels ascending and descending, could represent Jacob's needs and prayers ascending before God, and God's help and answers to prayer descending upon him. The ladder illustrates the connection between heaven and earth. Jesus said to one of His followers, Nathanael from Cana of Galilee, "Most assuredly, I say to you, hereafter you shall see heaven open, and the angels of God ascending and descending upon the Son of Man" (John 1:5). Jesus would have been referring to this story of Jacob's ladder, and saying that this ladder represents Him, for as He said, "I am the way, the truth and the life, No one comes to the Father except through Me" (John 14:6).

No doubt Jacob was aware of the prophecy concerning him that his mother received even before his birth, but not until this time did he have the covenant and all the promises (which had been given to Abraham and Isaac) personally confirmed by God Himself. Despite his unworthiness and sins, he heard the merciful and forgiving voice of God which gave him the courage to carry on. After awakening, Jacob made a vow with conditions before the Lord; if the Lord was with him in his going, provided all his needs and brought him back to his father's house in peace (meaning peace with his brother), then the Lord would be his God.

The Lord did indeed do for Jacob what he had asked, but these are things the Lord had already promised to do (28:15) and would have done, so these conditions expressed Jacob's lack of faith and carnality. However, his vow to give a tenth of all he had unto the Lord was commendable, and it must have been pleasing to God. This principle of tithing goes throughout the Bible and we, if we desire to please the Lord, should vow to tithe to Him as well.

We see the guidance of the Lord when Jacob arrives in his uncle Laban's territory. Providentially, Rachel went to the well much earlier than usual with her father's flock, arriving at the same time as Jacob. So the first person he met from his relatives was Rachel, his future wife. She was very beautiful and it was love at first sight. Laban had agreed to give her in marriage to Isaac after he had worked seven years for him. Then we see how the deceiver himself was deceived. In those days, the bride kept her face completely veiled and, unaware that he'd been tricked, Jacob married the older sister Leah. Laban used the excuse that in their country the younger is never married before the elder. However, after the seven days of the wedding celebration were over, Jacob took Rachel to be his wife as well and had to work an additional seven years, but because of his great love for her, the years seemed but a few days (29:20).

Jacob did not choose to become a polygamist, he was deceived into it. Polygamy was common in those days, and although the Bible does not command directly against it, the Bible does teach against it through examples of the many problems and evils it has caused. Jacob paid for his deceptions by getting a wife he did not love and by working hard and enduring afflictions (31:40-42) like a servant for his father-in-law for twenty years. The Lord saw that Leah was unloved and so he opened her womb. She conceived and gave birth to four sons (four tribes of Israel).

There is a biblical principle that, "whatever a man sows, that he will also reap" (Galatians 6:7). Jacob certainly reaped the deception he had sown to his brother and father. Let us be careful to be honest in all our dealings.

Prayer for today: *Almighty God, please give us Your grace of honesty in our confessions unto You and in our dealings with ourselves and others.*

Read Genesis 30 *January 17*

Key Verse: Genesis 30:22 *"Then God remembered Rachel, and God listened to her and opened her womb."*

God, as the giver of life, is the One who is in control of opening or closing wombs. Sarah, Rebekah, Leah, and Rachel were all barren, but God, in answer to their prayers, opened their wombs so they could conceive and bear children. When they did have children, it was evident to all that they were gifts from God. Children are truly gifts and blessings from the Lord.

When Rachel saw her sister Leah bearing children, she became jealous and cried out in desperation for Jacob to give her children. She was crying out to the wrong person, for even Jacob confessed that it was God who had kept her from bearing children (30:2). Then we find that, Rachel gave her maidservant, Bilhah to Jacob so that she might "have children by her", actually meaning to be "built up by her" (30:3). In those ancient cultures, if the maidservant bore a child for her mistress, the child would be considered a legitimate child of that mistress and her husband. Bilhah had two sons for her. Yet Rachel was not fulfilled; she had a burning desire and a longing to give birth and nurse a child of her own. She turned to the superstitious belief that eating mandrakes (a small orange-yellow fruit with a pleasant herbal smell about the size of plum, which grows in the wild) would bring her fertility, so she took them from Leah and, in exchange, agreed for Leah to sleep with Jacob that night. "God listened to Leah she must have prayed, and she conceived and bore Jacob a fifth son" (30:19), then again she bore a sixth son, and then her seventh was a girl, Dinah.

Rachel still was barren, but then she finally cried out in prayer to the right Person and we are told, "God listened to her and opened her womb". Finally Rachel conceived and gave birth to her long awaited son, Joseph, who became the greatest of his brothers. He was godly and used by the Lord, and Joseph became one of the most respected men in the Bible.

Once again, Jacob was back to his old tricks. He worked an extra six years for his father-in-law's livestock, but deceived him and ended up taking the strongest of the cattle. However, Laban confessed that since Jacob had been with him, the Lord had blessed him.

In this passage, we have seen the blessedness of children in the home, for they are "a heritage from the Lord" (see Pslam 127). In today's society, it is not viewed in the same way, thus the marriage institution has become degraded in many respects. Rather than wives desiring and being in the home to raise the children, we find many couples who do not even want children since they can be a "nuisance". We believe the main reason for this is lack of trust and commitment to God. Couples would rather remain selfish and work hard within the society than to work hard at building a strong family life. Many do not want the responsibility that goes along with having children, but as we have learned, children are a gift from God and He will also give the means to take care of them. Our whole society, including believers, needs the spirit of repentance because of our deviation from godly ways.

Prayer for today: *Thank You, Lord, for Your gift of family. Grant us Your strength so that we may glorify You in our family.*

Read Genesis 31 January 18

Key Verse: Genesis 31:3 *"Then the Lord said to Jacob, 'Return to the land of your fathers and to your kindred, and I will be with you'."*

Finally, after 20 years in Mesopotamia among the household of Laban, it was time to go home. Jacob heard from the Lord that he was to go back to the land of his fathers, and God identified Himself as the "the God of Bethel", the same God who appeared to him in a dream and reaffirmed the covenant with him. In doing this, the Lord also reminded him of the vows he had made, and thus far God had done as Jacob had asked and even more, for he not only had food and clothes, but great wealth and a large family. It was a good time for him to leave, since Laban and his sons showed animosity toward Jacob. When people put too much importance on gaining wealth, this becomes the root of covetousness, envy, and all evil (1 Timothy 6:10).

Jacob consulted his wives and they agreed to leave with him since their father had treated them unfairly as well (31:15). He took the first opportunity to secretly leave. When Laban returned and heard of their sudden departure, he gathered a group together and overtook Jacob in the hill country of Gilead. Laban was very angry, not only about their sneaking away, but also about the missing household idols. He could have caused them harm and taken away the livestock, but God spoke to him in a dream warning to "speak to Jacob neither good nor bad" (31:24).

The same God who interacted in increasing Jacob's wealth was now protecting him and his possessions. We can see that Laban was not only greedy and a deceiver, but a hypocrite as well, "I might have sent you away with joy and songs..." (31:27).

The household idols that Rachel stole are called "teraphim" in Hebrew. It is not clear what their purpose was but it has been suggested that they were important family heirlooms involving the inheritance. Possibly Rachel felt that since she was leaving everything, she deserved some part of the inheritance from her father (cf. 31:14), and these would have been very valuable. Like her husband and father, she was a clever deceiver, so her father did not find the teraphim.

Jacob and Laban made a treaty, not out of friendship but out of fear for each other. They put up a pile of stones as a sign and a border, agreeing they would not cross it to harm each other.

Jacob had left Canaan empty-handed, but we have seen how God helped him to prosper in the foreign land, and blessed him with many children so that at the time of his departure he had eleven sons and a daughter along with many servants and livestock.

Jacob's fear of Laban was unfounded, for after God had given him the direction to leave, He promised that He would be with Jacob (31:3). God did indeed protect him from Laban, for He always keeps His promises. This was something Jacob had yet to learn. But now the real fear for Jacob was to face his brother Esau, who had wanted to kill him. God can turn people to our favour when we follow Him and do as He commands. We need to trust fully in our loving God. "Therefore humble yourselves under the mighty hand of God, that He may exalt you in due time, casting all your care upon Him, for He cares for you" (1 Peter 5:6,7).

Prayer for today: *O Great God, we humble ourselves before You and trust You for the fulfillment of Your promise to take care of us and lift us up.*

Read Genesis 32 & 33   *January 19*

Key Verse: Genesis 32:10 *"I am not worthy of the least of all the mercies and of all the truth which You have shown Your servant..."*

When Jacob came to the border of the Promised Land "the angels of God met him" (32:1) and so he called that place "Mahanaim", meaning "dual camp". We believe he called it a dual or double camp rather than just a plain camp because it was special: it was the Lord's camp. Often in the Hebrew text, the dual or plural form of words are used in a singular sense to express majesty. This manifestation of the glory of God came after Jacob had overcome the fear of Laban, but he was still in more fear to face his brother Esau. In order to give Jacob confidence and joy, God allowed him to see a host of angels encamped as a mighty army, which may have been sent to Jacob to assure him that the Lord was with him to protect him and his family.

Still, Jacob remained in fear of his brother. When he heard that Esau was coming with 400 men, he became terrified. He thought they were coming as enemies and, still not trusting completely in God, he devised a plan to divide all his family and possessions in two companies so that if one was attacked the other might escape. Finally, Jacob does what he should have done first; he fervently prayed with a humble heart. In his prayer he acknowledges God as the personal living God of his father and grandfather, and he casts himself upon His mercy. He recognizes his condition is unworthy of the kindness and faithfulness of God, confesses his fear and asks God to deliver him from Esau. However, he might still have been depending on himself and lacking trust in God when he sent generous gifts to Esau at different intervals, so that his brother might forgive him and have his anger appeased.

One night, when Jacob was alone, possibly meditating and praying, he had a life-changing experience which could be called his conversion, for since that time Jacob, the "deceiver", was never like that again, and God changed his name to "Israel", meaning "Prince with God". "A Man wrestled with him until the breaking of day" (32:24). Take note that it was not he who instigated the wrestling, it was the Man that came to him. The reason for this might be to show Jacob that it was God who gave him the strength to persist and continue in the match.

Even after the Man struck Jacob's hip, putting it out of the joint and thus weakening him, Jacob was still able to wrestle. Now he learned that his weakness was made perfect in God's strength (2 Cor. 12:9; Hebrews 11:34; Joel 3:10). Jacob was given the fortitude to continue until dawn and would not let the Man go until he blessed him. He recognized it was a divine encounter and the blessing he desired was a spiritual blessing since, as we know, he was already blessed greatly in the material sense. Indeed, Jacob "struggled with God" (32:28), and the "Man" with whom he wrestled was most likely Christ in a pre-incarnate form (a Christophany). We know that Jesus Christ was always present, even in creation (John 1:1-5). The way Jacob prevailed serves as a great example for us to keep on in fervent prayer until we are divinely touched and blessed by God. We see in this story how God deals with His children in love, discipline and refining, to bring them to a point where they could be called "princes with God".

When Jacob first saw Esau, he approached him humbly, bowing down to the ground and prostrating himself before him, which was an ancient custom for one seeking to be granted forgiveness. But his brother Esau ran to him with hugs and kisses. They wept together and had a wonderful reunion after being apart for 20 years. No doubt God had intervened to change Esau's heart towards him. This had not happened because of all the gifts that Jacob had sent, for Esau did not even want them: he also had been blessed materially, and only took them after Jacob insisted.

Jacob, as a new man, now traveled with confidence, for he knew the Lord was his strength, so there was no reason for Esau to leave some men with him as protection (33:15). Also, after he had bought land in the Promised Land, he erected an altar to the Lord and called it "El Elohe Israel", meaning "God, the God of Israel" (33:20). For the first time we see Jacob now renamed Israel, calling the God of his fathers as his own personal God.

Prayer for today: *God of our fathers, we call upon You to restore broken relationships, keeping us in Your perfect will. Grant that we may not stop praying until we have Your assurance of blessing.*

Read Genesis 34 & 35   *January 20*

Key Verse: Genesis 35:2 *"And Jacob said to his household and to all who were with him, 'Put away the foreign gods that are among you, purify yourselves, and change your garments'."*

The first recorded incident of rape in the Bible was with Dinah, the daughter of Leah and Jacob. This is a tragic story of sin. Dinah was probably about 15 years old when she was violated by Shechem, the son of the ruler in that area. A shameful scandal had come upon the family of faith. Hamor tried to make the situation end for good by having them marry, which Shechem desired, then the two groups could live together like one family. The sons of Jacob dealt deceitfully with them and said they would agree if all the males among them became circumcised. Shechem was happy to do this if he could then have Dinah for his wife, and his father agreed and convinced his people to do this also.

Three days after the men were circumcised and in much pain, Dinah's two older full brothers, Simeon and Levi, took matters into their own hands and slaughtered not only the guilty, but all the men in that town. They stole their goods, and took away the women and children. They deceived those who had made peace with Jacob, thus upsetting their father and causing him to be hated by the peoples of the land. Jacob was afraid of what might befall him and his household because of his sons' wickedness. Although he is included with the men of faith listed by the writer of Hebrews (Heb. 11:21), here he was lacking in faith, for God had promised him many times to preserve him. Although Jacob's group were but "few in number" (34:30), all the surrounding cities had "the terror of God" upon them and so they were afraid to pursue the sons of Jacob.

Simeon and Levi were not punished immediately for what they had done, nor do we hear of Reuben's punishment for laying with his father's concubine, Bilhah (35:22), but these sins were remembered in Jacob's final blessings and prophesies over his sons (Genesis 49:5-7). Reuben lost his birthright as the first born son, and it was given to Judah. Simeon and Levi were to be scattered throughout the land, deprived of an inheritance. The tribe of Levi later came to be more godly than the rest, so they were chosen as priest of the Most High God, and although their inheritance of land was lost, they were scattered for a reason, to serve the Lord amongst the other tribes and "the Lord God of Israel was their inheritance" (Joshua 13:33).

The way God dealt with the Levites shows His mercy and forgiveness. The same is true for us today: if we are paying the consequences of sin, we can turn and be obedient to the Lord and ask for forgiveness, and He will forgive us, as He has promised (1 John 1:9; Isaiah 43:25), and turn the consequences of sin into a blessing.

Jacob was told by God to go to his father (who was in the southern part of Canaan, in Hebron), but he stopped short and set up camp in a place he should not have been. Sin always follows if one, in disobedience to God, is in the wrong place. God told Jacob to "go up" to Bethel. Although Bethel is south of where they were, it is located on a hill and to get there one must ascend about 305 meters. Bethel was where Jacob had seen the heavenly ladder, about 20 years before, and where God first spoke to him and made the personal covenant with him. Now, in returning there, Jacob ordered a family purification so they may go up to the "house of God" and have spiritual renewal and a time of revival. They had to be purified and told to "put away the foreign gods that are among you" (35:2). All things that hinder a close relationship with God must be buried and forgotten (35:4), then God will speak to us. God blessed Jacob and reconfirmed that his name would now be "Israel" and reaffirmed the covenant and promises which He had given to Abraham.

We are told of three deaths in chapter 35: the first was Deborah, Jacob's mother's nurse; then his beloved wife Rachel, died in giving birth to his 12th son whom she called "Ben Oni" (meaning "the son of my sadness") just before she died, but Jacob renamed him Benjamin (meaning "son of my right hand"). Finally, upon reaching Hebron, Jacob went to his father as God had commanded him. Isaac, at 180 years old, was dying. Esau also came to see his dying father. It must have made Isaac's heart glad to see his blessed son return to the land of promise, and to see Esau and Jacob reconciled. God honoured Isaac and may have let him live that long so that he could witness all this with his own eyes. With his heart at peace, Isaac died.

Prayer for today: *O God and Father of our Lord Jesus Christ, give us grace to put away anything that would displease You. Change and purify us we pray.*

Read Genesis 36 & 37   January 21

Key Verse: Genesis 37:3 *"Now Israel loved Joseph more than all his children..."*

We see in the genealogy of Esau that he was indeed blessed and that he himself became the father of a great nation. He could have sat around and sulked because of losing his birthright and blessing to Jacob, but he did not waste his time. He must have worked hard to become very wealthy. Somehow, with time and mainly by the doing of God, Esau's hate for his brother disappeared. He acted honourably when he met Jacob on his return to Canaan, and he again was honourable in that he moved from Canaan (although he was established there first) when the land could not support their combined livestock, in order to allow Jacob to remain in his Promised Land (36:6,7).

The Lord rewarded Esau for his goodness and blessed him greatly. From his line came a mighty people who had kings even before a king reigned in Israel (36:31). Esau's descendants came to be known as the Edomites. They lived in and around the area of Kadesh, in the northern part of the Sinai Peninsula. Now that Esau's line was recorded, the book of Genesis dismisses him and goes on to conclude about the family of Jacob (now called Israel), and the life of Joseph in particular.

Joseph was Israel's favorite son. He was the son of His most loved wife, Rachel, who conceived after God miraculously opened her womb. Israel gave Joseph a beautiful coloured garment which was usually worn by the eldest who had the birthright. His older brothers were obviously very jealous. Possibly Israel had decided to give Joseph the birthright and the blessing, but God had a different plan for Joseph's life.

Joseph was given dreams from the Lord in which he saw his future glory. He was only seventeen when he, perhaps unwisely, told his brothers that in these dreams they bowed down to him. The dreams probably served to comfort Joseph in his later distress. He also angered his brothers because he brought his father news of the wrong things they had done. Joseph was a righteous son and obedient to his father. His father loved him the most and showed favoritism towards him, so his brothers came to despise him.

The brothers had taken the livestock about 128 Kilometers away, to the area of Shechem. Since that was the area where Simeon and Levi had massacred those in the settlement of Hamor, their father must have worried about them and feared for their safety. He sent Joseph to check on them, and when they saw him coming, wearing his coat of many colours, they had the perfect opportunity to deal with him. Although Rueben, who as the eldest and took responsibility for Joseph, tried to save him, his plan did not work, for unbeknown to him, they sold Joseph as a slave to a caravan of Ishmaelites traveling to Egypt. When Rueben found this out, he tore his clothes to express his anguish and worried about what would happen to him when his father found out (37:29,30). They deceived their father into thinking that Joseph was killed by a wild animal. In those days many large wild animals (lions, or other large cats, or bears) roamed throughout Canaan. Israel was terribly grieved, almost to the point of death (37:35). Joseph ended up as a slave of Potiphar in Egypt.

God, however, had everything in control, and the terrible things that happened to Joseph were nonetheless all in His plan and purpose. Sometimes we do not understand why we go through difficult times. We cannot see what lies ahead, but God does. When Joseph was sold as a slave, and taken to Egypt, little did he know that one day he would be in charge of the whole country, second only to the Pharaoh himself. For the child of God everything that happens is a part of His plan. We must sometimes patiently endure pain or hardships, but

Jesus Christ said that in Him we can have peace for "In the world you will have tribulation; but be of good cheer, I have overcome the world" (John 16:33). There certainly is victory in Jesus!

Prayer for today: Lord, grant us the gift of grace so that we may trust You for the present and for the future.

Read Genesis 38 & 39   January 22

Key Verse: Genesis 39: 2a,9c *"The Lord was with Joseph, and he was a successful man;... How then can I do this great wickedness, and sin against God?"*

In the middle of the account of Joseph's life there is an interruption recording the sins of Judah and his sons. Why would these strange stories be written at this point and what are their significance? Later biblical prophecy and history revealed that Judah was the most prominent tribe among the Israelites, his was the royal tribe and the one from which the Messiah would come; therefore, it was important to relate the life of Judah and his sons.

Judah left his brothers and godly father, took a Canaanite wife and lived among them. She bore him three sons before her death. The first, Er, married Tamar, but we are told the Lord killed him because of his great wickedness. Judah was in the wrong place, and so many difficulties followed him. He did not instruct his sons in the way of the Lord, nor did he have a godly wife, so he lost his sons because of sin. If parents do not raise their children to love and serve God, they could lose their children as well.

Tamar was left a widow without children. This was an awful position for her to be in. At that time, and as it still should be today, the children were responsible to take care of their elderly parents. If the widow was left without children, it was the responsibility of her late husband's brother to marry her and thus give her a son to carry on her late husband's name and be his heir. Surprisingly, almost 500 years later, this same law was given to the children of Israel by Moses. (see Deuteronomy 25:5-10). Judah's second son, Onan, must have had something against his brother, Er, or else was very selfish, for he was not willing to give her a son who would inherit the double portion that should have gone to Er, the eldest son of Judah. Selfishness displeases the Lord, therefore he also was killed.

Judah promised his third son to Tamar, but maybe out of fear that he also would die, she never got to marry him. Judah lied and did not carry the responsibility he had toward her, so she deceived him into thinking she was a prostitute. Judah had fallen into the ways of the sinful society in which he lived and went to the prostitute. When God's ways are not followed, the sinful world's ways can be an trap. Thus Tamar conceived and in such a way Judah had two more sons, twins named Perez (who was the ancestor of King David, Ruth 4:18-22) and Zerah. They are all listed in Matthew's genealogy of Jesus the Messiah (Matt. 1:1-3). In spite of such sin, the grace of God was manifested, for these were the ancestors of Jesus.

When we return to the story of Joseph, we find a great contrast between him and Judah. God had given him success in all that he did. Surely he kept in mind that God was in control, so he accepted his position as a servant and slave, and did his job well and faithfully. Potiphar recognized this and made Joseph the head of the affairs of his household. While Joseph was with him, he also was blessed with great success and prosperity. Joseph was a very handsome, strong young man, with unusual leadership and courage. He sets a worthy example by his purity and strength of convictions. When Potiphar's wife made continuous sexual advances toward Joseph, he always resisted temptation and recognized it as a sin against God (39:9). In fact, one time he actually ran from the temptress (see 2 Timothy 2:22), but she held onto his coat and falsely accused him.

Although he was thrown in prison, Joseph nonetheless had the victory, for he remained pure in the sight of God (see 1 Peter 2:19). Most probably Potiphar knew he was innocent, but since it was an embarrassing public situation for him and his wife, he kept Joseph in prison. Joseph suffered there (Psalm 105:18), but he must have kept trusting in the Lord to bring him through, for he continued to show himself faithful and dependable and was even put in charge of all the prisoners. Keeping in communication with the Lord and having daily fellowship with Him keeps us pure with our eyes on Him so we may walk in the right way. Joseph would have done this and so we are told that the Lord was with him (39:23) and this was the secret of his success (see Matt. 6:22,23).

Prayer for today: *Holy Father, we recognize that all sin is against You. Forgive us and grant us the strength to take the way of escape from temptation which You always provide.*

Read Genesis 40 & 41:1-36 January 23

Key Verse: Genesis 41:16, 25b *"So Joseph answered Pharaoh, saying, 'It is not in me; God will give Pharaoh an answer of peace... God has shown Pharaoh what He is about to do'."*

Joseph was always aware of God and kept the faith of his father, even in a distant country, far from his family and the worship of the true God of Abraham, Isaac, and Jacob. Learning about God in his childhood played a great role in his life. It gave him the strength, knowledge and love for God in order to stay true to Him. Teaching a child in the way he should go is very important, for as the Bible says, "when he is old he will not depart from it" (Proverbs 22:6).

Joseph, though innocent and righteous, was suffering in prison, still the Lord had not forgotten him. When we are suffering and cannot understand why, we must remember that the Lord is still with us and he will bring us through, all in His good timing. Doing what is right does not always bring an immediate reward; in fact, it can sometimes bring suffering, as in Joseph's case. However, the Lord is faithful and just, and the good we do will not go unrewarded (Luke 6:35). For two years Joseph waited patiently in prison. When the time was ripe for the Lord to deliver him, He brought him out, putting him in an even better place than before.

We read that Pharaoh's butler (or cup bearer) and baker had "offended" him (Hebrew word for sinned), and he threw them in prison. One morning, Joseph, who was in charge of the administrative affairs of the prison, noticed their sadness and inquired about the cause. During the night, they both had dreams, but there was no one to give them the interpretation. Joseph knew that God was in control of everything and spoke boldly saying, "Do not interpretations belong to God?" (40:8). With faith that God could use him, he asked them to tell him their dreams. The interpretation for the cup bearer's dream was good, for he was to be restored. Joseph asked that he remember him before Pharaoh; however, he forgot him, but not totally. When the baker heard the cup bearer's good interpretation, he was anxious to hear his own. Joseph, having a pure and simple heart, was not afraid to speak the truth as the Lord gave him the interpretation. The baker would be hung in three days. Both interpretations came true.

When Pharaoh had two perplexing dreams, none of the trained magicians or wise men could interpret them. These were educated people who practiced fortune telling and studied astronomy. They even displayed unusual powers (but not from God) as in the story of Moses with Pharaoh's magicians who, like Moses, also turned their staffs into snakes. Pharaoh's dreams had come from God, and only those who know God have spiritual insight from Him to interpret what comes from Him. Pharaoh was desperate to discover the meaning of the two dreams he had. The cup bearer, wanting to help Pharaoh, remembered Joseph.

This was in the perfect timing of the Lord for Joseph to come out of prison. If he had been released earlier, he might have returned to Canaan, but God knew he was to remain in Egypt to fulfill His plan of salvation for him and his family. As quickly as possible Joseph, who was now 30 years old, was made ready for an audience with Pharaoh. Once again he gave the credit to God who is the revealer of truth (41:16). He told Pharaoh that the two dreams (two to emphasize the importance and urgency) have one meaning which God had chosen to show him concerning the seven years of famine which will follow seven years of plenty. Joseph wisely recommended to Pharaoh the course of action that should be taken. He did not show pride in himself for his abilities; rather, he was humble and knew that without the Lord it would be impossible.

We must remember that for all we have, whether talents, gifts or possessions, God must always receive the glory and hunour.

Prayer for today: *Father God, please reveal to us the knowledge we need in order to follow Your perfect will for our lives.*

Read Genesis 41:37-57; 42 *January 24*

Key Verse: Genesis 41:39 *"And Pharaoh said to Joseph, 'Inasmuch as God has shown you all this, there is no one as discerning and wise as you.'"*

The kindness and grace of God is beyond our imaginations. Probably no one else in history has risen to wealth and power in such a short period of time as did Joseph. When God exalts someone, He does it to the fullest. Joseph had given all the glory to God for his interpretation of Pharaoh's dreams, and Pharoah believed what Joseph had said as truth and confessed that it was God who had shown him and declared that Joseph was a man "in whom is the Spirit of God" (41:38). We are told in the book of James that if anyone asks God for wisdom, it will be given liberally (James 1:5,6). Pharaoh also exclaimed that Joseph was "discerning and wise" (41:39). We know that he was a man of faith and most assuredly he had prayed that God would give him wisdom, not only for when he faced Pharaoh, but for everyday life. Pharaoh gave Joseph the highest position under him in his kingdom, arrayed him in royal fashion, and paraded him through the city in a beautiful chariot with all the people bowing before him to show him honour (cf. Esther 6:7-9). Joseph's patient suffering was not in vain, for the Lord rewarded him. However, any earthly rewards we might receive are nothing in comparison to the coming heavenly rewards for faithful believers.

Joseph became fully integrated into the Egyptian culture. He was given an Egyptian name, and married an Egyptian girl, the daughter of the Priest of On. During the time of abundance, she bore him two sons whose names were significant in expressing the life of Joseph and, in naming them, God was referred to and given the glory. God is to be central in every area of our lives. We should continually think of Him and his praises should continually be on our lips (Psalm 34:1). Joseph's sons' descendants came to be included as a tribe among the children of Israel.

We see Joseph's cleverness, great wisdom, and extraordinary administrative abilities in his preparation for the famine. Again, God gave him success and favour, as He had done in Potiphar's home and in prison. During the seven years of plenty Joseph collected a huge quantity of grain. It has been suggested that there would have been enough gathered to last for 15 years, so in this way, not only Egypt could live during the famine, but many other countries as well. Just as Joseph had told Pharaoh, after seven years of plenty a great famine did indeed strike Egypt and the whole known world. Joseph's wisdom once again brought success and prosperity. Many people from other countries came to buy from him and so during this time Egypt would become tremendously wealthy.

Famines have always played a role in history. Abraham went to Egypt during a time of famine in Canaan, but the grace of the Lord brought him back to his land. There was another famine in the time of Isaac, but he was told by God not to go to Egypt, and because of his obedience, God blessed him greatly that year. With this great, extensive famine, God caused Joseph's ten brothes to leave for Egypt and be among those who came to buy from him. The dream Joseph had when he was 17 years old was now fulfilled when he was about 38 as they bowed down before him (42:6). After 21 years, Joseph would have looked quite different, shaven, speaking and dressing like an Egyptian, they did not recognize him. He spoke harshly to them, not out of anger or cruelty, but because he had a plan to test whether they were repentant for what they had done to him. He gave them a hard time, dealing with their consciences, so that they might have the fear of God in them and be reminded of how they had treated young Joseph. They did express their guilt and anguish for that sin and said what was happening to them was punishment for their evil deeds.

God, in his justice, never lets sins go unpunished, but He is also merciful and forgiving when there is repentance. Sometimes what may seem as a punishment actually works out for our own good so that we may come to repentance, without which there will be eternal punishment — a lot worse than any earthly punishment. When their father Jacob heard that Simeon had been left there in prison until they would bring the youngest brother Benjamin (Joseph's only full brother), he was in great sorrow, for after losing Joseph, he was not willing to let his precious, youngest son go.

Joseph was very wise in his dealings with his brothers. They were to become better people because of it. When we learn from our mistakes, we can increase in wisdom and the Lord can teach us many things.

Prayer for today: *Widsom, O Lord is Your gift to those who ask. We are asking and claiming Your promise to give wisdom liberally. (James 1:5)*

Read Genesis 43 & 44   January 25

Key Verse: *"Now therefore, please let your servant remain instead of the lad as a slave to my lord, and let the lad go up with his brothers"* (Gen. 44:33).

Jacob (or Israel) noticed the supply of food his sons had brought back from Egypt was almost depleted and, since the famine was still in the land, he told them to go down once more to buy food. Judah explained that because of the conditions set by the prime minister, it would be in vain for them to go without Benjamin. He promised his father he would bring him back, otherwise he would be forever guilty, implying a curse would be upon him. In need of food and to get Simeon back, Jacob agreed to let his youngest son (probably in his mid-twenties) travel to Egypt. Before they departed, he prayed to "El Shadai", the God Almighty, a prayer of protection over them. However he, lacking faith, ended with a note of pessimism (43:14).

When Joseph saw Benjamin had come with his brothers, he put his plan into action. Once again his brother bowed down before him, fulfilling his dream of long ago. Joseph was filled with emotion when Benjamin his only full brother, came to his home. He must have longed to go and immediately embrace him but restrained himself because he first wanted to see if his other brothers were changed and repentant. In fear, they spoke with Joseph's steward to express their innocence concerning the money that had been in their sacks on leaving after their first visit. The steward reassured them not to worry, speaking as though he were a believer in the true God. Joseph must have told the steward about the God of his fathers. The great news about our Lord is not something we should be quiet about. Others need to know!

46

Surprisingly, at the dinner the brothers found they were sitting in the exact order of their ages. Yet they had not figured out who the prime minister was even though he had asked them about their father several times, wondering if he was still alive. Then he showed favoritism to Benjamin, possibly to see how the others would react. Would they be jealous as they had been of him when he was shown favoritism by their father? No, they were happy and in good spirits (43:34), which might indicate a change of heart. But the real test was still to come.

Jacob could not accept money from his own father and brothers, so along with the food, he returned their money in the sacks as he had done the first time, but now he included his silver cup in Benjamin's sack. When it was discovered in his sack, the other brothers were terrified. To express their grief they tore their robes and went back to the prime minister. Joseph would not have practiced divination or fortune telling from his cup, but he was playing a role in a drama of which his brothers were not aware. Judah was the spokesman who, at first, was at a loss for words. Remembering their sin towards their young brother, Joseph, long before, he said, "God has found out the iniquity of your servants; here we are, my lord's slaves" (44:16).

Joseph, still acting, coldly replied that only the one who had the cup would be his slave and the others could "go up in peace" (44:17). They could not leave Benjamin or else their father would die. Judah, the leader and advisor for selling Joseph into slavery (37:26), had certainly changed. In Joseph's case, they had been cold-hearted and cruel, now they showed love and concern for their father and young brother. From the shock of all that had happened to them, their sleeping consciences were awakened. They saw their guilt and were sincerely repentant. Judah interceded on his young brother's behalf and asked that he remain as a substitute in place of Benjamin (44:33). We now see in Judah the spirit of self-sacrifice and true intercession, qualities which would become most evident in his descendant, Jesus, the Messiah. Joseph now was sure his brothers were changed. They had passed the test.

God loves you and wants what is best for you, and in everything the Lord has a purpose. God may use trials to teach us, convict us, and bring us to repentance. If you are in need of repentance, do not hesitate. The Lord is merciful and kind and willing to forgive.

Prayer for today: *Dear God, please help us to recognize that you allow testings in our lives in order to teach us important lessons for life.*

Key Verse: Genesis 45:7 *"And God sent me before you to preserve a posterity for you in the earth, and to save your lives by a great deliverance."*

The climax of this beautiful and touching story has arrived. After Joseph saw the changed hearts of his brothers, he revealed his identity. It was an emotional time, but Joseph's brothers seemed to be uneasy, "dismayed in his presence" (45:3). They were afraid he would repay them for the evil they had done to him. In spite of his many reassurances, they continued to be uneasy for many years (cf. 50:15). Joseph, however, truly forgave them. Rather than being resentful and bitter (which, without the love of God in his heart, would be considered normal), Joseph recognized the sovereignty of God. He told them several times that it was the plan of God for him to be in Egypt "to preserve life" (45:5). Joseph's wisdom did not only guide and help Egypt during the time of plenty and famine, but most importantly, his being there was to fulfill the purpose of God for his family to become a nation from which would come the promised Seed. The grace and mercy of God is incomprehensible! The Lord had planned for their salvation, just as He has also planned for yours through His son Jesus.

Joseph told his brothers to migrate to Egypt with their father and all their children and herds. There they would have plenty of food, for there were still five years of famine yet to come. His high position and prestige gave him the authority to let them dwell in the land of Goshen, which was ideal for grazing herds and yet was near to him in the fertile eastern delta area. Here they could shepherd their herds far from the civilized city of the Egyptians, who considered them an abomination (46:34). They were free to live as they pleased and to worship God in their own way, remaining separated from the heathen Egyptian culture. Before his brothers left, Joseph gave them gifts for themselves and extra gifts to Benjamin, along with gifts for his father. Pharaoh welcomed them to come and generously said all the goods of Egypt were theirs. He supplied them with carts for the children to ride in and it seems there was even a special cart sent by Joseph for his father Israel.

Upon seeing these Egyptian carts, Israel believed Joseph was alive and we are told his spirit was revived and he was willing to go so he could see Joseph before he died (45:27,28). It is interesting to note that when he was in doubt he is referred to as Jacob (45:26), but after believing, he is referred to as Israel, "prince with God" (45:28). On the way south, Jacob stopped at Beersheba to offer sacrifices to God where his father Isaac (26:25) and grandfather Abraham (21:33) had erected altars previously. Possibly Jacob hesitated about going, thinking of the bad experience Abraham had there and the fact that God had told his father Isaac not to go down to Egypt. He must have prayed for guidance and counsel from God. In a vision, he heard the voice of the Lord telling him not to be afraid, but to go to Egypt where God would make of him a great nation. The Lord comforted him by saying Joseph would be at his side upon his death, "Joseph will put his hand on your eyes", meaning Joseph would close his eyes in death. God gave Jacob seventeen more years of life after he arrived in Egypt (47:9,28). In the same vision, the Lord assured Jacob He would bring his family back again to the land of Canaan. The Lord is faithful, and what He has promised we must be confident He will do.

Prayer for today: *Thank You, Lord, for Your great provision for us. May we access daily Your storehouses of blessings for spirit, soul and body.*

Read Genesis 47 & 48 *January 27*

Key Verse: Genesis 48:21 *"Then Israel said to Joseph, 'Behold, I am dying, but God will be with you and bring you back to the land of your fathers.'"*

After Joseph's family arrived in the land of Goshen, he went with five brothers and his father and to explain to Pharaoh that they were herdsmen. Probably, Joseph, in his wisdom, had instructed his brothers what they should say to the king. Pharaoh showed them kindness and generosity and confirmed that they would live freely in Goshen. He even gave Joseph the authority to put one of his competent brothers as the chief herdsmen over his livestock. Pharaoh seemed interested to meet Joseph's father and with respect he asked him his age. Without any intimidation, Jacob spoke freely with Pharaoh and told him he was 130. Then we are told he blessed Pharaoh, which is amazing in light of Hebrews 7:7 which says, "And without doubt the lesser person is blessed by the greater" (N.I.V.). Jacob, who had a glimpse of God, spoke with God and heard from God, was the greater, for spiritual greatness is far more important than position or riches.

As the famine became more severe, we see how Joseph, with the gift of administration, wisely set the economic policy for the country. He may have seemed a little hard on the people, but he was truly concerned for them. He was doing his job well and fulfilling his obligations. Before long, all the livestock and land belonged to Pharaoh, for the people traded them for grain and seed after all their money was gone. Joseph wisely distributed the people all over the country, rather than having them concentrated in one area, so that more food could be produced. The people still tilled the land, keeping four-fifths of its produce and giving one-fifth to Pharaoh; yet, they were grateful to Joseph that they were still alive in the midst of such a famine (47:25) and everything he did was acceptable.

With these economic policies, Joseph brought tremendous wealth to Pharaoh and yet was fair to the people as well. We need to pray for those in leadership and government positions that they, like Joseph, will have wisdom and understanding.

When Israel knew he was close to death, he summoned Joseph to his bedside. In the same manner as Abraham had done with his servant (Genesis 24:2,3), he asks Joseph to put his hand under his thigh, thus making a solemn vow. Jacob asked Joseph to promise to bury him in the Promised Land along with his fathers in the cave of Macphelah. Joseph swore that he would. It seems that it was soon afterward that Joseph was once again summoned to his father's bedside. He brought along his sons, Manasseh and Ephraim, for it was important that his father bless them before he died. Israel, almost blind, saw dimly the figures of two men standing in the room and asked who they were. When he was told, he kissed and embraced them. They would have been in their early twenties then and Israel expressed thanks to God that He had brought him to even see Joseph's offspring, whom he claimed as his own sons, to be blessed and receive the promised inheritance, like his other sons.

With spiritual insight and the gift of prophecy, Jacob blessed the youngest with his right hand on his head, which is significant for it means he would receive the double portion of the inheritance and be greater than the older Manasseh. The history of Israel proved this to be true. In this chapter we see the great faith of Jacob (Hebrews 11:21), or we should say Israel, in God's covenant promises, and we see his sensitivity to the leading of the Holy Spirit. He repeatedly reminded them, without a doubt, they would return to the land of Canaan, their Promised Land. Over the years and through many hard experiences, Jacob finally came to have complete faith and trust in God. We have the men of faith in the Bible as examples to follow and we have the complete, final and full revelation of God in His Son and in His Word; therefore, we do not need to learn by trial and error (although sometimes in our stubbornness that is what it takes), since all the truth is set before us in the precious Holy Book.

Read Genesis 49 & 50   January 28

Key Verse: Genesis 50:20 *"But as for you, you meant evil against me; but God meant it for good ... ".*

This is a scripture verse which most clearly expresses the divine providence of God. It sometimes seems as though the evil people have the advantage over the godly, but in the end the plan and purposes of God will indeed prevail. Throughout the whole book of Genesis we see the providence of God over and over again.

Jacob, now 147 years old, called his sons to bless them and prophesy concerning their future "in the last days" (49:1). In their context this meant the days before the coming of the Messiah (that is, the first time when Jesus was born in Bethlehem). In the original language, his words are very beautiful, like a poem having rythmical movement, figurisms, clever play on words. Unusual expressions and parallelism all combine to make a warm, heart-felt monologue spoken as the Holy Spirit led him. He gave a great messianic prophecy: "The scepter shall not depart from Judah" (cf. Revelation 5:5), "until Shiloh comes", referring to the Messiah Jesus. "Shiloh" may mean "to whom it belongs" that is the scepter of the "lawgiver". This shows that Judah was to be the governing tribe of Israel (King David's line) and pictures the Messiah as the ultimate governor from that tribe, which was fulfilled in Jesus. It seems Jacob split the birthright between Judah, the ruler with spiritual leadership and recipient of the messianic promise, and Joseph's son, Ephraim, who would see national prestige, material blessing and success (Joshua, Deborah, and Samuel came from his tribe).

Judah had proven himself to be worthy in offering to be personally responsible for Benjamin (43:9) and in offering himself as a substitute for him (44:32,33). Historically, the tribe of Judah remained firm in the faith, even when the other tribes (except Benjamin) fell into idolatry during the reign of Jeroboam. In Jacob's blessings to his sons, we can see that the Holy Spirit guided his words so that he saw, by faith, the history of the nation. Jacob was speaking these things while on his deathbed and, in the middle of his discourse, it seems with longing that he says, "I have waited for your salvation, O Lord"

(49:18; cf. Isaiah 25:9; 1 Peter 1:10). He knew he was about to die any moment and may have been gasping for breath and looking by faith to that salvation which he foretold; "Shiloh" will come and subject all people.

After his blessings, Jacob told his sons that he was to be buried in Canaan and in giving details he made it very clear that they understood where the cave was in the field of Machpelah. Jacob lived a long life and possibly the best years were spent enjoying the bounty of Egypt with all his sons together in unity. The third patriarch, a great man in the Bible, died in peace with all his sons around him. Joseph fulfilled his vow and with much splendor, and accompanied by many Egyptians, Jacob's sons carried his body to its resting place in Canaan.

After Jacob's death, Joseph's brothers were afraid that he would take his revenge against them for what they had done to him. But Joseph kindly showed his brothers that he had truly forgiven them and promised to continue taking care of them. Joseph lived a consistently godly life. He walked faithfully day by day in the fear of the Lord. He had a peaceful life and lived to enjoy his great grand children (50:23). He, too, requested that he be buried in Canaan with his father and grandfathers, however, with faith he said they could take his bones with them when God brought them out (Hebrews 11:22; Exodus 13:19).

Joseph lived to be 110, and throughout his life he was used mightily as an instrument of God. We see in his life an example of faithfulness and trust in God whose will is good, perfect, and acceptable (Romans 12:2). Whether good or evil happens to us, God has a purpose for "we know that all things work together for good to those who love God, to those who are the called according to His purpose" (Romans 8:28).

Prayer for today: *O Lord, because You are our Lord, we trust You to work all things together for good in our lives, in order that Your purpose may be fulfilled.*

Introduction to
The Book of Matthew

I like the way Sherman E. Johnson begins his introduction to Matthew in the *Interpreter's Bible:*

"When a convert to Christianity in the late first century or early second century read the Gospel according to Matthew for the first time, he read it as a manual of membership rather than as a part of his Bible. It was one of the recent "best sellers" of Christian literature. A present day reader should be led to look at [Matthew], not as one who has had some acquaintance with it all his life, but as an ancient Christian into whose hands it has just come. This is a difficult feat of historical imagination, but it is worth attempting" (IB vol 7,p.231).

Matthew was a bit of a surprise as a best-selling author. Among other things, he was a Jewish tax-collector: a turncoat, plying his trade in Capernaum on behalf of the hated Romans. But Matthew was also a bit of a scholar. Much of his book relates to Old Testament scripture and its fulfillment in Jesus. Indeed, he sees Jesus as, without question, the long-hoped-for Messiah. And to Matthew, good Jew that he was, Messiah meant King.

As you read Matthew, try to think like that new convert in ancient days. Imagine yourself Jewish. Imagine yourself captivated by the Jewish scriptures with its promise of a Jewish Messiah. Imagine that your grandfather or great-grandfather has told you stories of a teacher from Nazareth who was crucified, with "King of the Jews" written above his head on the cross. And imagine you've heard of the empty tomb. Imagine all this, and Matthew will change your life, as you read of "Jesus Christ the King".

Read Matthew 1 & 2 *January 29*

Key Verse: Matthew 1:20 *"...that which is conceived in her is of the Holy Spirit"*

Matthew is the only one of the gospel writers who starts his record of the life and ministry of Jesus with a genealogy. Genealogies aren't fun to read. In fact, they can be downright boring, but Matthew seeks to clearly demonstrate that Jesus Christ was the Son of David and the Son of Abraham. He sees it important that Jesus comes from the line of men who had a special relationship in history with God and His plan. God gave a promise to Abraham, and He gave a promise to David. Jesus Christ, in Matthew's eyes, is the fulfillment of that promise. But once you get past the genealogies in verses 1 through 17 of chapter one, you get into the meat of Matthew's high view of Jesus Christ.

The key verse is verse 20. Jesus, although descended from Abraham and David, is unlike them in that there is a supernatural dimension in His life. Literally conceived in the flesh by the supernatural agency of the Holy Spirit, Jesus Christ is set apart from any other human being who has ever lived. So, right off the top, we have the history of a man who not only claims to be the Son of God, who not only rises from the dead and ascends to the Father later on in His life, but is also supernaturally conceived. In every sense of the word, He is the Son of God.

It's interesting that Matthew follows up this comment on Jesus' conception by recording the word of the angel in verse 21, "And she will bring forth a Son, and you shall call His name Jesus, for He will save His people from their sins." Jesus' function, His purpose, is that salvation come to the world. All have sinned, all need salvation. There is only one way for salvation to be achieved, and that's through the Son of God shedding His blood for the sins of the world. And so, when He says, "this was done that it might be fulfilled which was spoken by the Lord through the prophet," we see there is an historical continuum. Jesus comes to save people from their sins both now and in the future, in accordance with God's word to Israel through the prophets in history past.

Prayer for today: *Lord, thank you for Your great love that brought You down to become "God with us", not only then, on earth, but now in our hearts.*

Key Verse: Matthew 4:17 *"Repent, for the kingdom of heaven is at hand."*

After successfully dealing with Satan's temptations in the wilderness, Jesus began his ministry. His message was very straightforward, "Repent, for the kingdom of heaven is near."

I think we need to be clear about this subject of repentance. Confession of sin is not repentance from sin. Confession demands honesty — in many cases, brutal honesty. And hope lies in that honesty. But the fact is that one can be honest about one's sinfulness again and again and again and again. This is a problem that many of us face.

We're constantly confessing our sin but not repenting. Repentance means turning around and going in the opposite direction. Whereas confession demands honesty, repentance demands commitment — resolution plus follow-through. Repentance is very difficult and in some cases with those of us who have some kind of weakness, we may find ourselves repenting every day. The truth is, if we actively turn around from a sin before we commit it, then we find ourselves less and less in need of confession. That's not to suggest we become perfect, but nevertheless it is to suggest that we'll start growing. Something that's encouraging about repentance is that as we turn around and go in the opposite direction, the kingdom of heaven comes to meet us.

God is committed to the active repenter, and so we should be encouraged to make that choice, however difficult. By an act of our will, we choose to turn around from our sin. Obviously, from Jesus' point of view, repentance was and is absolutely vital. There is a relationship between repentance and the coming of the kingdom. A little later on, Jesus will be teaching His disciples to pray and He'll say, "Thy kingdom come." Now, a lot of us would rather pray, "thy kingdom go." When the kingdom comes especially near to us, there is a sense of the holy that will not tolerate sin. So "repent," Jesus says. If you want the kingdom of heaven to be near, turn around and go in the opposite direction of your sin, and as you do so, be assured the kingdom of heaven will not only be near, it will, in fact, come to meet you.

Prayer for today: *Help us to not only confess our sins to you, Lord, but to also REPENT, turning around and going the opposite direction as an act of our will.*

Read Matthew 5 *January 31*

Key Verse: Matthew 5:3 *"Blessed are the poor in spirit, for theirs is the Kingdom of Heaven."*

This beatitude not only sets the tone for Jesus' "sermon on the mount", but it's also the bedrock of Jesus' ministry. He came to bring men and women into the kingdom. It wasn't just a case of coming and announcing the kingdom; the hearers of that announcement had to willingly embrace the kingdom. There were requirements, repentances, commitments and obediences which were part and parcel of the meaning of embracing the kingdom. So, when Jesus says, "Blessed are the poor in spirit, for theirs is the kingdom of heaven," He's telling us that spiritual poverty is the general qualification for entry into the kingdom of heaven.

I think you and I might put it differently. We might say, "Blessed are the successful, the victorious, the pious, the religious and the spiritual giants, for theirs is the kingdom of heaven." We'd say this because all of us are guilty, to a greater or lesser degree, of the sin of pride. Pride is the antithesis of what Jesus is talking about here. Proud people tend to compare themselves with others and put down either the other person, or themselves. Putting yourself down, by the way, is not virtuous. Sometimes an inferiority complex is an inverted form of pride. We compare ourselves with others positively or negatively and then we compete with others. This can happen in fairly subtle ways. We attempt to rise above the other guy — to put him down if we can't rise above him — but in some way, to push ourselves ahead.

We also have this longing for unrestrained independence. We don't want to be dependent on anyone, God included. We try as much as possible to be self-sufficient. Well, poverty of spirit is antithetical to pride. To admit that one is poor in spirit is a humiliating and painful experience. We're not talking here about putting oneself down, rather we're talking about seeing oneself in the light of the kingdom of heaven, totally undeserving, totally dirty, totally incapable of entry because our garments are so unworthy. Jesus looks on those who acknowledge their poverty of spirit and says, "You are the ones I am looking for. I didn't come to call the healthy, I came to call the sick."

Perhaps the most important lesson of all for us to learn is that, even though we're made for the kingdom, the kingdom will never be ours until the day we honestly confess to God our unworthiness.

Prayer for today: *Thank you, Lord, for your boundless grace which gives us entrance into Your kingdom, though we are undeserving and unworthy servants.*

FEBRUARY

*The "Mount of the Beatitudes" on the North shore of Galilee.
The traditional site of Jesus' teaching recorded in
chapters 5, 6 and 7 of Matthew.*

Read Matthew 6   *February 1*

Key Verse: Matthew 6:9 *"This is how you should pray..."*

Jesus teaches us how to pray and I've often noted how simple this prayer is and how complex most of our praying seems to be in comparison. Like the pagan, Jesus says, we sometimes think we'll be heard for our much speaking, for our babbling, for our repetitions. They use many words, as He says in verse 7; not so with Jesus. He wants us to be short with our words and direct. So He gives a prayer lesson.

Just a few observations: First of all, the focus is our Father in heaven, which is the way it must always be in prayer. Before we start asking God for things, we've got to take time to remind ourselves of who He is and focus on His holiness and majestic transcendence. "Hallowed be Thy name, Thy kingdom come, Thy will be done." The focus is on Him, His name, His kingdom, and His will. As we concentrate first and foremost on Him, anything else that may follow in our prayer takes on a fresh and balanced perspective.

Sometimes our prayers are a knee-jerk reaction to a negative or urgent stimulus. And we "rush in" to tell God what He's got to do, and what we want, and how important it is He do it now.

Well, if you'll take time to focus in on Him, first of all, and see yourself in the context of His holiness, His plan for the kingdom and His will for your life, then some of these other urgencies become tempered and balanced. After this, you can focus on yourself. "Give us this day our daily bread. Forgive us our debts as we have also forgiven our debtors. Lead us not into temptation but deliver us from evil." We stress our physical and spiritual needs, our relationship needs and ultimately our eternal destiny needs. We must always remember in prayer that we are headed for an eternal kingdom — this very kingdom of heaven that Jesus makes the centre of His ministry. Thus, as we pray, we always begin with God Himself, focussing in on Him, praising Him, thanking Him, worshipping Him. And in that context, imploring Him to meet us at our point of need.

Prayer for today: *Lord, teach us to pray, even as You taught Your disciples, that we will focus on You first and then on our own needs.*

Read Matthew 7   *February 2*

Key Verse: Matthew 7:2 *"For with what judgment you judge, you will be judged..."*

He knows that it's as natural for humans to judge one another as it is to breathe. And every one of us is guilty. Every one of us is making judgments of others, as hard as it may be sometimes for us to admit it.

Jesus simply reminds us that when we are judging others we are, in a very interesting way, judging ourselves. Or at least He suggests that the intensity, the zeal, the inflexibility of our judgments will somehow be used against us. He is also suggesting that we often judge people for the very things of which we ourselves are guilty. So, in a sense, when we are judging others, we are judging ourselves. Maybe that in itself lends some intensity to our words. He reminds us that relative to other people's faults, our own faults are much larger, or at least appear to be much larger. Whereas a speck is simply a speck in someone else's eye, that same speck looks and feels like a plank in our own. And so as we scrupulously attempt to help our brother to improve, not only is our judgment thrown off by the fact that we can't see clearly due to the imperfection in our own eye, but we are also acting hypocritically if we don't remove that plank first.

Now it may seem rather strange that in this context Jesus then says, "Do not give dogs what is sacred. Do not throw your pearls to pigs." It seems like He is making some judgments or encouraging us to make some judgments right there, in calling some people dogs and pigs. I'd like to think that at this point in time, some little stray mutt came walking among the disciples and Jesus just keyed in on that by saying, "Hey, in this area of judging others, be discerning. Don't bare your heart to everyone. Don't give your treasure to everyone because not everyone can understand or appreciate where you're coming from or what it is you're giving them. Be discerning, be wise, be gentle."

Sometimes, in attempting to show our magnanimity and vulnerability, we merely invite hurt and misunderstanding. So, rather than being torn to pieces, be discerning in whom, and with whom, you share your heart, and save yourself a lot of sorrow.

Prayer for today: *Help, us, oh God, not to be judgmental toward others but to carefully judge ourselves to see how our lives line up with Your Word.*

Read Matthew 8 *February 3*

Key Verse: Matthew 8:34 *"And when they saw Him, they begged Him to depart from their region."*

The driving out of the demons from the two demon possessed men in the region of the Gadarenes has always received a lot of comment, because it's so spectacular. You know the story well. Jesus casts the demons into a local herd of pigs who then rush down into the Sea of Galilee and drown. But there are two things which stand out in this account.

First, the response of the demoniacs was, "What do you want with us, Son of God?" You wouldn't expect Jewish people to be confessing that Jesus is the Son of God. Much less would you expect demonic spirits to be confessing that Jesus is the Son of God. And yet they knew exactly what was going on. They knew who Jesus was and that something remarkable had happened in history, in God becoming flesh and dwelling among men. They don't pull any punches. They know exactly who Jesus is and they tell it like it is. Jesus is the Son of God. This is not the last instance where demonic spirits refer to Jesus as He really is. They live in the spirit realm and they have eyes to see what we here in space and time do not see. So we should take note of their insight, even though they tremble at the very thought of who Jesus is.

The second thing about the story is that the whole town, when they found out what had happened, went out to meet Jesus. You'd expect that they'd be so impressed with what He'd done that they would call on Him for salvation. No, rather surprisingly, they said, 'get out of here, please'. They pleaded with Him to leave their region. We have no account here of great evangelism or a turning to God. They just wanted to get Jesus out of there, fast. So here you have demonic spirits confessing that Jesus is the Son of God, and Jesus getting rid of them. And you have human spirits trying to get rid of Jesus.

Figure that one out!

Prayer for today: *We praise You, Lord, that even the demons recognize their powerlessness in Your presence, and because you live in us, we have the same authority over them.*

Read Matthew 9 *February 4*

Key Verse: Matthew 9:11 *"Why does your teacher eat with tax collectors and sinners?"*

Matthew, as we all know, was one of Jesus' disciples. In fact, he is the writer of the book we're now studying. But Matthew was one of the undesirables in Israelite society. He was a Jew, yes, but he was a tax collector for the Romans. In this position, he could demand whatever he thought a person was capable of paying, give the Romans whatever percentage they wanted, and keep the rest for himself.

A tax collector was seen as getting rich from the sorrow and oppression of his own people. To say he was despised was an understatement. He was down there with the prostitutes, drunks and criminals, the down-and-outers. So you would think it a bit of a public relations disaster that Jesus would call a tax collector to be one of His key followers, one of the twelve disciples. Yet that's exactly what He did. Jesus called this despised person to be one of His men. He goes to his house to have dinner to seal the bargain, and many of Matthew's friends are there — tax collectors and sinners — eating with Him and His disciples. Of course this was the stuff the teachers of the law and Pharisees loved to see to further emphasize their hatred of this teacher from Galilee. So they asked a question of His disciples, "Why does your teacher eat with tax collectors and sinners?" Jesus' response was, "It's not the healthy who need a doctor but the sick."

It's reminiscent of the Sermon on the Mount, "Blessed are the poor in spirit, for theirs is the kingdom of heaven." Jesus came to those who recognized their spiritual poverty. Self-righteousness and pride are always the effective blocks in any work of the kingdom of heaven in our lives.

Prayer for today: *Thank you, God, that You meet us where we are. Help us to be extensions of Yourself to those that the world despises.*

Read Matthew 10 *February 5*

Key Verse: Matthew 10:34 *"I did not come to bring peace, but a sword"*

In this chapter, Jesus sends out His twelve disciples. It's the first time He has invested them with a ministry responsibility and it's not difficult to see that He recognizes their greenness, their newness at this huge task of world evangelization. This is nowhere more evident than in the very first thing He says to them, "Do not go among the Gentiles or enter any town of the Samaritans. Rather, go to the lost sheep of Israel." Jesus recognized that the challenge of the kingdom was to the Jew first, then to the Gentile. But I'm sure He was also very aware that His disciples were in no condition at this point, in terms of their spiritual maturity, to tackle the awesome challenge of ministering a Jewish message, indeed a Jewish messiah, to a Gentile people. There would be a communication gap to say the least.

So Jesus challenged them to preach the Kingdom to the lost sheep of Israel. In that context they're to heal, to raise the dead, cleanse the leper, drive out demons. And they're to do it in a way that doesn't expect any financial reward. As you read the chapter, you can see the tremendously high view that Jesus had of His disciples. You also get a remarkable insight into His own self-limitation.

You'll remember on another occasion, recorded in Mark 13:32, Jesus says that no one including the angels and Himself, the Son, knows the time of the Day of the Lord. The only one who knows is the Father. This perhaps would help us to understand verse 23 where He says, "You will not finish going through the cities of Israel before the Son of Man comes." I think it's entirely possible that Jesus, in His self-confessed ignorance, thought it was entirely possible that the culmination of history would occur very soon.

Nevertheless, He saw the commissioning of the disciples as the giving of a sword to His men. He recognized that they would, with their message, turn a man against his father, a mother against her daughter. In other words, divide families. And looking at them, He says, "If you love your father or mother or anything else or anyone else more than me, you're not worthy to be my disciple." He's really impressing upon them the urgency of the hour and the message they are to bring.

Prayer for today: *Lord, may we feel the same commissioning the disciples were given and sense the urgency of the hour, giving us spiritual fervency.*

Read Matthew 11 February 6

Key Verse: Matthew 11:28 *"Come to Me, all you who labor and are heavy laden, and I will give you rest,"*

In this chapter, we have two contrasting sides of Jesus' ministry portrayed. First of all, He very bluntly and directly condemns Chorazin, Bethsaida and Capernaum, cities that were not repenting of their sin, not listening to His message of the kingdom. He's telling them that Tyre and Sidon would have been much more responsive to the gospel message than these cities; that is, the Gentile cities would have heard Him, whereas the Jewish cities seemed to ignore Him. He warns them that it will be more bearable for Sodom on the day of judgment than it will be for them. But then, secondly, He turns around and says that He is grateful to His Father in heaven that He has hidden the realities of the kingdom from the wise and learned, and revealed them to little children.

Jesus heart is obviously moved by the gentle souls, the spiritually impoverished ones who humbly and shyly approach Him. As He looks about and sees these dear ones, these weary, burdened and tired people, He says, "Come to Me, I'll give you rest. If you are going to work, take My yoke upon yourself rather than the yoke of the world. Understand that I am not a hard taskmaster but in working with Me, who am gentle and humble in heart, you will find rest for your souls. My yoke is easy, my burden is light." In some ways, you might wonder at this, in that His disciples lived stressful lives, and in some cases met untimely and violent death. On the other hand, that inner peace, that peace that passes understanding, that sense of security, that sense of destiny, of being a part of a greater plan, is such an overpowering and overwhelming thing that earthly stresses and strains are put into perspective. How else can we explain the seeming joy and peace of the martyrs throughout the centuries who have gone to their deaths praising the Lord? How else do you explain those who have lived a life of poverty and deprivation for the sake of the gospel, not asking anything for themselves? Obviously, Jesus is onto something here. He knows something that we should know and it's this: we have been created for eternal life and should be looking to the far horizon to discover the real meaning of life and the focus of our souls.

Prayer for today: *Oh God, may we realize that when we come to You, we find rest for our souls, even in the midst of our earthly stresses.*

Read Matthew 12 *February 7*

Key Verse: Matthew 12:8 *"For the Son of Man is Lord even of the Sabbath"*

This is the first of what are known as the Sabbath controversies in the gospels. On this occasion, Jesus' disciples were picking some heads of grain and eating them as they walked through some grain fields on the Sabbath day. The Pharisees, who were always looking for a chance to accuse Jesus of unlawful behaviour, pointed out that the disciples were doing what is unlawful on the Sabbath. Jesus responded by referring to an historical event when David entered the house of the Lord with his companions and ate the consecrated bread which was lawful only for the priests to do. He establishes the fact that the Sabbath is something which should serve man rather than man serving the Sabbath. He then informs these men that He is the Lord of the Sabbath, and offends them even more.

Later that day, Jesus happened to run into a man who had a paralyzed, shriveled hand. Again, the Pharisees were there looking for a reason to accuse Him, and so they asked Jesus if it was lawful to heal on the Sabbath. He replied, "If you have a sheep who falls into the pit on a Sabbath, won't you take hold of it and lift it out? Well, a man is much more valuable than a sheep. Therefore, it is lawful to do good on the Sabbath."

So, in terms of these Sabbath controversies, Jesus established two things. First of all, He is Lord of the Sabbath, which gives Him the authority to declare what is lawful and what is not; and secondly, what is lawful is to do what is good and, of course, doing good is something which can involve work. Jesus says, "If it's good, do it." Now, it was good to heal a man, so He healed him. "Stretch out your hand," He said, and it was completely restored. The Pharisees couldn't handle this, and they went out to plot how they might kill Jesus.

In terms of the twentieth century, it is good for us to remember that any institution we may have and hold dear is good only to the extent that it serves us. When it comes to the point where we're serving it, then, like the Pharisees, we may have made more of the institution than Jesus Himself would ever make of it.

Prayer for today: *Lord, may we seek to do good, even at the risk of going against the grain of societal norms and institutions. You are Lord of all!*

Read Matthew 13 *February 8*

Key Verse: Matthew 13:11 *"It has been given to you to know the mysteries of the Kingdom of Heaven..."*

In this chapter Jesus tells one of His better-known parables, that of the sower. Most parables have only one point and they generally make it well. The major point of this one parable comes in the form of a question, "What kind of soil are you?" Only a small amount of seed which is broadcast over the ground will eventually bear good fruit. The disciples responded by asking, "Why do you speak to people in parables?" And Jesus' answer seems to be rather strange. "It's in order that most will not understand what I'm talking about". In the context of the parable, however, it becomes a little clearer. The parable says that only a small percentage of those who hear will respond and bear fruit. If that is the case, then the quality teaching, the kind of teaching that will "grow in grace and knowledge", that will "grow from faith to faith", is intended only for those who have ears to hear. So those who are able to see will see.

Jesus was not about to waste a lot of good stuff on unreceptive hearts. He's teaching about the kingdom here. This is not evangelism. Evangelism is the broadcasting of the seed; no question about that. But when it comes to the indepth ministry of the spirit, the parable is constructed so that only those who are members of the kingdom will have the interest and the commitment to try and get beyond the metaphor to discover, as the spirit enlightens them, what it is Jesus is really saying.

The parable of the weeds follows very naturally the parable of the sower. First of all it's similar imagery, but secondly, in terms of what Jesus had just said about broadcasting seed and then speaking through parables, this parable of the wheat and the weeds shows us that Jesus was not about to form an exclusive club in His presentation of the kingdom. He was prepared to broadcast it generally to all men everywhere and, in fact, was prepared to allow the members of the kingdom to grow up surrounded by those who are not members. He was not about to pull His disciples out of the world and form a commune: He wanted them in the world.

Prayer for today: *Thank You, Lord, that You reveal to us, through Your Word, the "mysteries of the kingdom". Help us to broadcast seed (Your Word) and may it fall on good ground.*

Read Matthew 14 *February 9*

Key Verse: Matthew 14:27 *"Be of good cheer! It is I, do not be afraid."*

Matthew takes a moment to tell us about Herod and his beheading of John the Baptist, then he gets into the remarkable miracle of the feeding of the five thousand. Jesus, who was involved in a very people-intensive ministry, seemed to have limitless capacity for giving out more and more, and showing a kind of inexhaustible compassion, to the point of actually and miraculously dividing five loaves of bread and two fish into enough to feed five thousand. But then, He also has the self-confidence to be able to dismiss the crowd. He gets into a boat and goes to the other side of the lake just to get away from them. He eats and runs!

After Jesus dismisses the crowd, He goes up by Himself into the hills to pray. Jesus placed priority again and again on quiet time with His Father. While He's praying, His disciples are out on the lake. Suddenly they look up and see Jesus walking on the water. Their first reaction is, "It's a ghost!" But Jesus speaks to them and says, "Take courage. It is I. Don't be afraid." And Peter, the impulsive fellow that he is, says, "Lord, if it is You tell me to come to You on the water." Jesus says, "Come." Peter gets out and walks on the water toward Jesus. But then, half way there, he realizes what he is doing and, beginning to sink, cries, "Lord, save me!" It would have been interesting if we had seen Peter walking all the way to Jesus and then turning around and walking back to the boat with Him. But, on the other hand, there is something refreshingly human about Peter's reaction.

The response of the disciples to Jesus walking on the water is, "Truly, You are the Son of God." And truly He was. When they got to the other side of the lake, the people there recognized Jesus and sent word to all the surrounding country, and brought all their sick to Him and begged Him to let the sick just touch the edge of His cloak. And all who touched Him were healed.

Notice the human context out of which Jesus' ministry sprang. He dealt with hungry people, frightened disciples and needy, demanding miracle seekers. His ministry sprang out of the very stuff of human existence.

Prayer for today: *It is with great relief, Lord, that we find the disciples were as human as we are, yet You used them so mightily. Use us, oh God, as Your strength is made perfect in our weakness.*

Read Matthew 15   *February 10*

Key Verse: Matthew 15:28 *"O woman, great is your faith! Let it be to you as you desire."*

This is a strange story, to say the least. It's a story of a Canaanite woman whose daughter was demon-possessed, who came to Jesus crying out for mercy that her daughter might be healed. Apparently she was so insistent that the disciples became upset and urged Jesus to send her away. Jesus' response is what makes the story so difficult. He answered, "I was sent only to the lost sheep of Israel." Now it appears that He's being uncharacteristically callous and hard. But notice that His disciples were there, and they undoubtedly remembered that He had already sent them out to the lost sheep of Israel. They knew this woman was not one of those. They knew she was a Caananite, a Gentile, one often referred to by Jewish people as a dog. And perhaps in order to appear consistent to His disciples, He said what He said, but then, probably looking at the woman with tongue in cheek, as it were, He said, "It is not right to take the children's bread and toss it to their dogs".

The woman, instead of being intimidated by this statement, which may have been a quotation of a popular saying, responds almost as though it is a game, saying, "Yes Lord, but even the dogs eat the crumbs that fall from the master's table." There's obviously some kind of repartee going on between Jesus and this woman. There's a non-verbal communication that the disciples miss. How else does one explain her remarkable wit and self-assurance? She obviously read in Jesus' look a compassion, an empathy, an openness that she very quickly siezed. Jesus used her as a tremendous object lesson saying, "Woman, you have great faith. Your request is granted," which is reminiscent of the centurion who had greater faith than anyone in Israel. The thing that jumps out here is the fact that Jesus refused to be painted into a corner, even by His own words. He has a marvellous flexibility about Him and a kind of youthful adaptability that took as it's rule, first and foremost, the rule of love.

Prayer for today: *Lord, You know us so well; You know exactly how to deal with us to boost our faith, trust and growth in You. May we respond to Your promptings as did the Canaanite woman.*

Read Matthew 16 & 17 February 11

Key Verse: Matthew 16:16 *"You are the Christ, the Son of the living God."*

In chapter 16, Jesus asks His disciples, "Who do people say the Son of Man is?" And the answers were predictable. "Some say John the Baptist, others said, Elijah, some said Jeremiah or one of the prophets." "But what about you, who do you say that I am?" And it's good old Simon Peter who answers, "You are the Christ, the Son of the living God." This is a great confession of faith, and Jesus replies, "Blessed are you Simon," and He comments that this was not revealed by man, but by God the Father in heaven. It's at this point Jesus says He'll build His church on this rock, on this confession of faith; and as long as the church believes that Jesus is the Son of the living God, then that church will be well-founded and the gates of hell will not prevail against it.

In that context, those who are a part of the church, especially of its leadership, will have authority on earth and in heaven, in terms of fellowshipping with, or disfellowshipping, individuals who may or may not be a part of the kingdom of heaven in that church on earth. But then Jesus does something very strange. He warns His disciples not to tell anyone that He is the Christ. The only thing that comes to mind here is that it wasn't time yet for the general populace to hear about this. He then talks to the disciples about what He's going to face before it's finally revealed who He is. And as Jesus talks about His trials, His sufferings, His death and resurrection, Peter says, "Never Lord, this shall never happen to You." Jesus turns on Peter, just after commending him, and rebukes him, "Out of My sight, Satan, you're a stumbling block to Me."

Why this strong reaction? Maybe it's because this was almost like a fourth temptation to Jesus. And so Peter is almost like Satan here in terms of his tempting Jesus to avoid the issue and find some other way to establish His Christness in the public domain. It's just another indication again of the remarkable hybrid that is man. We're very much part of the earth, and at the same time the image of God which is in us has such heavenly potential. On the one hand, we can make great confessions of faith, and on the other hand, act as agents of the devil.

Prayer for today: *Lord Jesus, we too can exclaim with the same zeal as Peter, "You are the Christ, the Son of the living God!" May we have similar zeal in telling others.*

Read Matthew 18 *February 12*

Key Verse: Matthew 18:3 *"Unless you ... become as little children, you will by no means enter the kingdom of heaven."*

Even the disciples had egos. This must have been at the root of their question, "Who is the greatest in the kingdom of heaven?" Like you and me, they would want to hear Jesus say, "Frankly, in all honesty, you are." And even as we humbly accepted it, we would be privately glowing, with smug joy at our special status. Well, Jesus characteristically surprised them all. He brought a little child, stood him among them and said, "You must become like a child or you'll never enter the kingdom of heaven. Whoever humbles himself like this child is the greatest in the kingdom of heaven. Whoever welcomes a little child like this in My name, welcomes Me."

The last thing an adult would expect is to be told to regress to childhood. What's the point? It is simply this — a child recognizes authority. A child is forever learning, has a boundless enthusiasm, innocence, and malleability that an adult just doesn't possess. And Jesus goes on to say that anyone who misleads a child is going to be in big trouble. More than that, Satan's going to be in big trouble because of the stimulus he has provided to sin in mankind.

Jesus then turns to His disciples, changing pace somewhat, and says that if their foot or their hand or their eye causes them to sin, they should cut it off or gouge it out, or somehow maim themselves in order to avoid sinning.

Certainly, Jesus is not expecting a bunch of disfigured and dismembered disciples to be following Him about. He is, as He often does, using exaggeration for the sake of emphasis, but the point He's making is clear. Sin is a serious thing. And even as a child is relatively sinless, so too we must approach the kingdom of heaven with that kind of innocence — an innocence which comes not from self-generated righteousness but from a committed belief in Jesus Christ as Saviour and Lord.

Prayer for today: *We come to You today as little children — humble, teachable and full of trust. Take our pliable lives and shape us, Father, into the image of Your Son.*

Read Matthew 19 & 20   *February 13*

Key Verse: Matthew 19:30 *"But many who are first will be last, and the last first."*

A rich young man comes up to Jesus and says, "What must I do to get eternal life?" Jesus' response is a little strange. He says, "Why do you ask Me about what is good? There's only one who is good." The initial impression is that this is a bit of a put down. But then again, maybe Jesus is just trying, as He often does, to shock His listener into attention by saying what He least expected to hear. He then gets into the expected answer. "If you want to enter life, obey the commandments." He asks which ones, and Jesus says such and so. And the young fellow says, "I've kept all of these." Jesus then tells him that if he wants to become perfect, to go, sell his possessions to the poor, and then he'll have treasure in heaven. Well, the young man left him sadly, because he had a lot of money.

At this point, Jesus uses the opportunity to teach His disciples that it's very difficult for a rich man to enter the kingdom of heaven. The disciples want to get a little deeper into this. In fact, they're greatly astonished and ask, "Well then, who can be saved?" And Jesus says, "Naturally speaking, in the human realm, it's impossible to be saved. Only with God is it possible to be saved." Peter says, "Look, we've left everything to follow You. What's going to be in it for us?" Jesus then tells them that whoever has left houses or brothers or sisters or father or mother or children or fields, will receive one hundred times as much and will inherit eternal life.

Then He throws in a disclaimer. Many who are first shall be last, and many who are last shall be first. This is, perhaps, to avoid any attempt on the disciples part, or on ours, to reduce entry into the kingdom of heaven to a legalism such as: if you leave what's valuable to you, or sell what is valuable, you're guaranteed eternal life. Jesus says, "Not necessarily so." A lot who appear to have done all this, in God's eyes still will be lost. And many who have appeared to have neglected this, will be found. Obviously, He's telling us, among other things, that what He said to the rich young ruler was a specific instance and shouldn't be overly generalized.

Prayer for today: *Your ways, oh Lord, are so much higher than ours. Thank You that You're in control and know best, even when Your ways conflict with our earthly values.*

Read Matthew 21 February 14

Key Verse: Matthew 21:22 *"And whatever things you ask in prayer, believing, you will receive."*

This chapter includes a tough passage. First of all, it seems uncharacteristic of Jesus to be going about cursing trees, especially trees, as Mark tells us, that are out of season, Secondly, even though we're accustomed to Jesus using hyperbole (that is, exaggerating for the sake of emphasis), as any good Semitic teacher and rabbi would do, we are thrown by His reference to physical mountains being cast into the sea, and anything being received that is asked for in prayer with faith.

What is Jesus really telling us here? "If you have faith and doubt not, or if you believe, you'll receive whatever you ask for in prayer." The promise in its very form excludes a literal fulfillment. The phrase, "to remove mountains," was a natural exaggeration and Jesus is referring to the mountains of difficulty that we face every day in life; but to refer to Mount Hermon, as likely this mountain indicates, just gave a greater vividness to an illustration which the disciples could easily understand. A mere physical miracle, such as Mount Hermon being thrown into the Mediteranean, would never in itself be the object of faith as Jesus describes it. The exaggeration is meant to impress on the disciples' mind the truth that lies beneath it.

When Jesus says that belief will see you receiving whatever you ask in prayer, there is the implied condition, as we see in chapter 7, that what is asked is in harmony with God's law and God's will. In fact, if it weren't in harmony with His law and His will, it wouldn't be asked in faith. Every true prayer involves submission to God's will in the matter. This is why we need to be very careful with a passage like this, that we don't use it as a springboard to irresponsible praying, or prayer as a means to a worldly end.

We must always submit what it is we ask to the greater issue of God's will for our lives and the world and commit ourselves in a childlike way to whatever He chooses to do.

Prayer for today: *Grant, dear Lord, that as we continue learning how to pray, Your Holy Spirit will guide us to pray according to Your Will and not ours.*

Read Matthew 22 *February 15*

Key Verse: Matthew 22:21 *"Render therefore to Caesar the things that are Caesar's, and to God the things that are God's."*

Here we have one of the most famous stories about Jesus, when He comments on giving to Caesar what is Caesar's and to God what is God's. What is fascinating about the story is that the Pharisees and the Herodians got together in attempting to trap Jesus in His words. These two groups had very little to do with one another, and in fact represented totally different political points of view. The Pharisees tended toward ardent Nationalism, the Herodians toward cooperation with the growing force of occupation. So the Pharisees would be against paying tribute to Caesar, but the Herodians would be for it. Yet here they were, working together. Both the religious and the political establishments saw Jesus as a threat.

Jesus' response to the question is anger, "you hypocrites, why are you trying to trap Me?", and then tremendous cleverness, "show Me the coin used for paying the tax." (I think it is interesting Jesus didn't have a denarius to His name.) The next question is simple, "whose portrait is this? whose inscription?" "Caesar's", they replied, then followed the famous answer.

Jesus refused to align Himself and His message with any kind of zealous nationalism. Though He claimed to be Israel's leader, He denied any kind of kingship which was focused only on temporal and political power. The kingdom that Jesus represented was one in which everything is God's. This meant that even though one rendered unto Caesar that which was Caesar's, all of those monies and political infrastructures would ultimately fall under God's dominion.

It's a good point. Especially for those of us who associate

Christianity with capitalism and the west. God is working powerfully in communist countries in the east. He's not subject to our political idealogies and divisions, for He is Lord of all.

Prayer for today: *Thank You Lord, for Your infinite wisdom. As Solomon of old prayed for wisdom, so do we, that we might communicate Your truth in tough situations, as Jesus did with a hostile crowd.*

Read Matthew 23 *February 16*

Key Verse: Matthew 23:39 *"Blessed is He who comes in the name of the Lord!"*

This chapter has been entitled "The Seven Woes" by many commentators, because seven times Jesus pronounces woe on the Pharisees. There's no need to expand on the various criticisms that He has of the Pharisees, because the main point of the seven woes is in verse 3, "do not do what they do for they do not practice what they preach". Jesus' criticisms are about doing righteous things to be seen by man. He also addresses the misplacement of authority in calling various Pharisees "Rabbi", "Father", or "Teacher". Does this mean we're wrong to be calling anybody "Teacher" or "Professor" or "Master" or "Father"? No. In the context, Jesus is essentially flattening the spiritual pride He sees in the Pharisees and the titles they assume for themselves. He talks about their zeal to win converts and yet their blindness as guides. He talks about their ability to teach the Law and yet their inability to perform it. He also talks about the fact that He is going to send prophets, wise men, and teachers, to try and steer the Pharisees in the right direction, but predicts they will be killed and crucified just like others before them.

It's in this context that Jesus weeps over Jerusalem. He uses the powerful imagery of a barnyard hen clucking a warning as her little chicks rush to nestle under her wings for protection from some intruder. It's a very pastoral, loving, and compassionate picture. When Jesus, however, was "clucking", the chicks were not running. Because of their inattention, their temple was going to be left to them desolate. Then He says, "I am going to be gone too." Which only adds to the desolation.

Israel won't see Jesus again until they say, "Blessed is He that comes in the name of the Lord". Here we have a reference to the end of days and the developing doctrine in the New Testament of the second coming of Jesus Christ and His triumphant reign as Messiah.

72

Read Matthew 24 *February 17*

Key Verse: Matthew 24:42 *"Watch therefore, for you do not know what hour your Lord is coming."*

The subject of the end of the age is something that has been written and preached about to the point where one wonders if anything original can be said. So there's no need to delineate all of the various details of this chapter and speculate as to their possible fulfillment, but there are a few things that jump out at you.

It starts with the disciples asking Jesus the question of what will be the sign of His coming and the end of the age. Jesus responds by mentioning four things: #1 There will be many people claiming to be Christ. #2 There will be all kinds of wars, famines and earthquakes. #3 The whole world will hate the believer and #4 the Gospel will be preached to that whole world as a testimony to all nations.

In the framework of those four things, Jesus says we're not to be alarmed at the false prophets, and we should understand that the wars, famines and earthquakes are just the beginning of birth pains. We should also remember that, even while believers are being hated by all nations, the one who stands firm to the end will be saved. And as far as the Gospel of the Kingdom being preached to the world is concerned, the end won't come until the whole world has heard the message. Jesus then speaks of several other factors contributing to the end of the age. But He stresses again something He has said before — that no one knows the day or hour, not even the angels in heaven nor the Son, but only the Father. Jesus does not emphasize end-time agenda or time frame here, although He does say that the generation which sees all of these things (especially the preaching of the Gospel to the whole world), will not pass away until all of the things that have happened culminate in the coming of the Kingdom.

The key word in this chapter is in verse 42, "Keep watch". Stay alert. Keep your brain in gear. Keep your heart tuned to the voice of the spirit and expect the coming of the Lord at any time.

Prayer for today: *In these last days, oh Lord, we pray that we will be ever ready and watching for Your return at any moment. May we never slumber and miss this glorious event.*

Read Matthew 25 *February 18*

Key Verse: Matthew 25:23 *"...you have been faithful over a few things, I will make you ruler over many things."*

The parable of the ten maidens is very much a one-point parable. Jesus had just talked to His disciples about the signs of the times and the importance of keeping watch in anticipation of the coming of the bridegroom. Here is a parable which stresses again the importance of keeping watch. It is simple but profound. Jesus tells all who anticipate the coming of the Bridegroom, all who are looking forward to the coming of the King, that they should stay alert because we don't know the day or the hour, and in that lack of knowledge, we should be expecting Him at any time, any day, any moment.

The parable of the Talents is also a simple parable stressing the point that God expects us to use the talents He gives us. Sitting on them, neglecting them, or being resentful if you didn't get more, is to abuse what God has given you; and not to employ an opportunity means to lose it. The truth seems to be, if you don't increase, you somehow decrease. Perhaps Jesus was also suggesting that His people had been entrusted with the Law and the Prophets and all kinds of gifts from God. If they can do no more than put the deposit of faith into some kind of legalistic safety deposit box, then somehow they may run the risk of losing their special privileges.

There is a warning here that is universal in scope, not just to Scribes and Pharisees, but to all to whom God the Holy Spirit has revealed Himself. We recognize that He has given us His gifts, invested us with talents, not just that we be gifted, but that we contribute to the Kingdom wherever we may be. So, in terms of the "Signs of the Times", Jesus challenges us to be alert, informed, involved and ready. He's at the door.

Prayer for today: *Thank You, Father, for giving all of us individual abilities and talents. We pray today that we will be found faithful in using them to advance Your kingdom in Jesus' name.*

Read Matthew 26 *February 19*

Key Verse: Matthew 26:11 *"You have the poor with you always, but Me you do not have always."*

This chapter is the beginning of what is known as the passion narrative — the story of the arrest, trial, crucifixion, and resurrection of Jesus Christ. It begins with Jesus Himself predicting that at the

Passover He would be handed over to be crucified. It's at this point the chief priest and the elders of the people plot to kill Jesus, but they don't want to do it during the feast of unleavened bread, which begins at the Passover, because they feel that there would be a riot among the people.

Nevertheless, the plot begins and the tension and speed of the narrative starts to pick up. It opens with a very unusual event in Bethany where Jesus is in the home of Simon the leper. Simon was probably someone whom Jesus had healed from leprosy. A woman, unnamed, comes to Him with an alabaster jar of very expensive perfume and pours it on His head as He reclines at the table. The disciples, like all good Christians everywhere, were angry because this perfume could have been sold at a high price and the money given to the poor. Jesus responded by saying this was a special event — "The poor you will always have to minister to, Me you will have only for a short period of time." He goes on to say, "When she poured this perfume on My body, she did it to prepare Me for burial".

It could be that the woman thought she was forcing Jesus to claim the kingship because anointing on the head was something that was done to kings. It could be she thought that by doing this she might spur Jesus into some kind of action. What He did was turn the act into something else. He said that she may have thought she was anointing Him to be King, but in fact she was anointing Him for burial. It was a very poignant moment: one that Jesus said would be remembered wherever the Gospel was preached throughout the world. Nevertheless, He would not allow anyone, however loving and loyal he or she might be, to force Him to fulfill any agenda other than that of His Father in heaven.

Prayer for today: *We praise You Jesus for the way You followed the will of Your Father, unswayed by the world, even unto death on a cross. We pray for the determination to imitate You, our perfect example.*

Read Matthew 27 & 28   February 20

Key Verse: Matthew 28:6 *"He is not here; for He is risen, as he said."*

The account of Jesus' resurrection is foundational to Christian faith. In fact, all of New Testament theology presupposes resurrection, and Paul, in 1 Corinthians 15, says that if Christ is not risen, our faith is in vain. Why? Because if Christ be not risen, then the central point of His teaching is in question. He says that He is the Son of God, and as such He should be able to rise above mere human mortality, as human as He was. If He, like us, is mastered by the grave, then however kind, good, loving, and miraculous His ministry is, He is just like any other man.

We read there was a violent earthquake and an angel descended, rolled back the stone and sat on it. His appearance was like lighting, his clothes were white as snow. The guards were so afraid that they shook and became like dead men; possibly lying unconscious in their fear. Mary Magdalene and the other Mary came along. They had seen Jesus die, had witnessed His burial, and now they witnessed the empty tomb. The angel told them to bring a message to the disciples that Jesus would meet them in Galilee. Hurrying away, they suddenly encountered Jesus. As they clasped His feet and worshipped Him, Jesus said, "Don't be afraid, go tell My brothers to go to Galilee and there they will see Me."

Don't be afraid? Who wouldn't be afraid at a time like this? Never before had something like this occurred. That's part of the legitimate lesson of Resurrection Day. Resurrection Day should inspire a certain kind of fear. One theologian said that we live in an enclosed valley called earth and Easter takes us to a neighbouring height to show us a world vaster than we have dreamed. It's true!

Resurrection Day gives us an insight to the world that is to come. It brings a gripping historical confirmation to Paul's theology which tells us that Christ is the firstfruits of them that shall also rise, meaning you and me and all believers everywhere throughout history. We have a destiny, and we will individually be glorified and recognizable one to another. We will no longer be subject to death and decay. We will follow where Jesus has led us. That empty tomb is an open window to the kingdom of heaven.

Prayer for today: *Hallelujah, You are risen! You are alive and have conquered death, giving us the blessed hope of being with You in glory on the next resurrection day.*

Introduction to

The Book of Exodus

Moses, as an eye-witness, records historical facts in the book of Exodus. It is a truly amazing story of God's redemption of Israel out of bondage from Egypt (in about 1445 B.C.) and their becoming a free nation in a covenant relationship with Him. The theme of the book is the redemption and covenant of the Lord with Israel. How privileged and honoured they were to be chosen by God to become the nation through whom the promised Messiah would come into the world. In fact, within the book of Exodus there are more types (pictures) of the Person and work of Jesus Christ than in any other Old Testament book, for as Jesus said concerning Himself, "he [Moses] wrote about Me (John 5:46). The tabernacle, priesthood, sacrifices, and even Moses as their mediator of the covenant, of reconciliation and communion with God, all have much symbolism pointing to Jesus Christ. Often it is found that knowledge of these things in the Old Testament helps in understanding the New Testament (and vice versa).

In the Hewbrew language, the book of Exodus is named by the first two words of the book, "we'elleh shemot", meaning "and these are the names", but it is more commonly referred to as "shemot", "Names". The word "and", sometimes translated as "now", shows that it is a continuation of Genesis, the first book of Moses. The Greek Jewish translators named the book "Exodus", meaning "a going out" or "a departure"; taken from Exodus 19:1, which is the main topic for the first part of the book, dealing with Israel's departure from Egypt. Although Israel physically departed from Egypt early on in the book (14:30), in their hearts they never really left until they repented of their sin in worshipping the golden calf toward the end of the book (33:4). Then, with the renewal of the covenant, Israel was restored and in actuality this was their exodus from the sinful world, and thus they were set apart as the Lord's people and then set free and delivered by His grace.

Read Exodus 1 & 2 *February 21*

Key Verse: Exodus 2:23b, 24 *"Then the children of Israel groaned because of the bondage, and they cried out; and their cry came up to God...and God remembered His covenant with Abraham, with Isaac, and with Jacob."*

This is an amazing story about the providence of God. There is a gap of over 400 years between the death of Joseph and the birth of Moses (a descendant of Levi). During this time, the family of Jacob grew incredibly fast to become a nation that was so numerous that the Egyptians feared them. The new king was not God-fearing and he possibly was from a different dynasty, so he was unfamiliar with the goodness of Joseph in saving Egypt. Filled with anger, he gradually forced greater and greater hardships upon them until they became Egypt's slaves. Under such ruthless oppression, history tells us that thousands of people have died. Yet, God did not want this to happen. He was faithful in keeping His promises to the Patriarchs, so the Hebrews continued to grow and multiply. Satan has always tried to kill and devour and, through Pharaoh, he tried to destroy the people of God so they would not become a great nation through whom the Messiah would come. But the will of God always prevails. When Pharaoh ordered the midwives to kill the Hebrew newborn baby boys, they did not obey him for they feared God more than Pharaoh (1:17). Because they obeyed God and did His will, they were rewarded (1:21). May God help us today to follow His will rather than Satan's, and see the end of abortions — the killing of innocent babies.

The children of Israel may have thought God had forgotten them, but "God heard their groaning". Even before they cried out to Him, He was planning their deliverance in His perfect timing. When Moses was born, he was a beautiful child and his godly mother must have sensed that God had a great plan for his life. By faith she hid him for three months (Hebrews 11:23). By faith she made him a little ark and, trusting that God would keep him from harm, she set him afloat on the Nile river (in which he was supposed to be thrown to drown, 1:22). God can even use the ungodly to accomplish His plan. Pharaoh's own daughter (the right person) came (at the right time) to bathe (at the right place) and, by the leading of God, found Moses amongst the reeds. It is truly amazing that at the climax of Pharaoh's anger and desire to kill the Hebrew boys, God, in His providence, had Moses growing up in Pharaoh's own home and being raised as a prince where he had opportunities to learn about leadership, so he could eventually lead out the children of Israel. Then, because of his education he was to write the first five books of the Bible, the Torah (Acts 7:22).

When Moses murdered the Egyptian, he wrongly took the deliverance of his people into his own hands (cf. Acts 7:25). He did this out of the spirit of nationalism, which was the wrong motivation (later on we see positive motivation in Exodus 32:32). This was not God's way, nor was it the right time for God to deliver them. However, the Lord used this incident to send him into the wilderness to learn for 40 years in the school of God.

Moses took a Midianite wife, Zipporah, the daughter of Reuel (meaning "friend of God"), the priest of Midian (area south-east of Sinai). The Midianites were godly descendants of Abraham through his son Midian by his wife Katurah, whom he married after Sarah died (Genesis 25:2). Reuel and his family kept the faith of Abraham and worshipped the One true God (Exodus 18:12).

The Lord accomplishes His plan faithfully, for He will always do what He promises. Their time of bondage was fulfilling prophecy, but God had promised to bring them out and this was their hope. God accomplishes His plan through people, even unlikely people such as Pharaoh's daughter. He accomplishes His plan providentially through circumstances. The baby Moses needed someone to nurse him, and the Lord brought his godly mother back to him so he would know his heritage and be taught in the ways of the Lord. God accomplishes His plan victoriously as we see in His eventual deliverance of the children of Israel.

You are very valuable in God's eyes, and He wants to accomplish His plan through your life. Our hearts and minds should be open to His leading.

Prayer for today: *O Lord, as Israel cried out to You for deliverance, so we cry for the deliverance of the people of our generation from all bondage. May Your plan be fulfilled.*

Read Exodus 3 & 4 *February 22*

Key Verse: Exodus 3:4 *"God called to him from the midst of the bush and said, 'Moses, Moses!' And he said, 'Here I am.'"*

A time of preparation under the training of God is important before one is ready to do the task that He has prepared. Moses went from being a prince to being a humble shepherd. This must have broken any self-pride he may have had. Spending 40 years as a shepherd (like his forefathers) in the wilderness must have enabled him to have many quiet times with the Lord. The best years of anyone's life are spent with God. The first 40 years of Moses' life were beneficial, but the second 40 years were necessary. All the wisdom of Egypt was not enough to make him a servant of God; he required the time for devotion every day, just as we require this to serve God in the way we should.

God had planned to send Moses on a great mission, but before that He had to appear to him and speak to him directly from the burning bush. This was the method the Lord used to attract Moses, then He called him, equipped him, sent him and used him. When God spoke, Moses was in His presence and so he was required, out of respect for the holiness of God, to take off his shoes, for wherever the Lord is, is holy ground. To hear from the Lord and be in His presence believers must remove from their lives that which is unholy, for God cannot be glorified where there is unholiness.

God not only revealed His holiness on Mt. Horeb, but showed His grace by revealing that He was a living God who saw the affliction of His people and who was preparing a land for them, just as He had promised Abraham. Mount Horeb, or Sinai, was the starting point of Moses' ministry, and it was from this same mount that God later revealed Himself to him in a fuller way (34:5-7). Moses lacked confidence in himself and also lacked faith in God, as is evident in his questions and excuses. He asked "Who am I?" (3:11) to do this job. It seems it was not said out of humbleness, but rather from a feeling of inferiority. He had doubt in himself. God assured Moses that He would be with him and this should have been enough to give him confidence, but it was not. If God be with us, nothing will be impossible and who can be against us (Romans 8:31)? Moses, out of fear, continued to raise objections. God answered all his questions and gave solutions to his excuses.

Moses lacked knowledge about God and so God gave him the knowledge he needed. He told Moses His name, "I AM WHO I AM". This expresses the richness and fullness there is in God. He is the way, the truth, and the life (John 14:6). This is the same name Jesus used for Himself (John 8:52). The great "I Am" is our righteousness, holiness, redemption, provider; He is our everything.

Moses then expressed another difficulty in doing the task, and this was a fear that the people would not believe him. Therefore, God provided him with miraculous signs to prove he was sent by God. Again, this should have been sufficient to convince him and take away any fear or doubt, but the human heart is often slow in belief. It is amazing to see how patient and gracious God was to him. God demands obedience from His children. He knows if we are capable to accomplish a certain task, or He would not have called us. And those He calls, He also enables and equips by His strength, power, and might. We read that the Lord is slow to anger (Psalm 103:8), but when Moses refused, saying God should send another, that was the "boiling point" (4:13,14). Moses, though weak, could have accomplished the task with the strength of the Lord. But because of his stubbornness and lack of trust, God gave him Aaron, his brother, to be a partner and a spokesman for him. Moses finally agreed.

The Lord will never make you do anything that is against your will, but He will provide what is needed for you to follow His will. Once Moses knew God's will, he and his family set out for Egypt. On the way, the wrath of God was upon him because he had not circumcised his son. Those in the work of the Lord are to do His will and be obedient in every area. Concerning the matter of circumcision, those children of Abraham who did not obey it were to be "cut off from his people" (Gen.17:1-22). How then could Moses be their spiritual leader and not obey God in this important sign which set them apart unto Him? After obeying, he and Aaron went with faith to their brethren in Egypt, who believed in his call from God upon seeing the signs from the Lord. Signs and miracles follow the believer today, just as they did with Moses and Aaron.

Prayer for today: O Great "I Am", we humble ourselves before You. Grant us grace to trust and obey You always.

Read Exodus 5 & 6 February 23

Key Verse: And Pharaoh said, "Who is the Lord, that I should obey His voice to let Israel go? I do not know the Lord, nor will I let Israel go." (Exodus 5:2)

After God's divine manifestation of signs caused the people to believe and worship Him (4:30,31), Moses and Aaron, filled with encouragement and faith, went before Pharaoh. Most probably to their surprise, Pharaoh refused them the three day leave to worship and sacrifice to their God. Pharaoh's attitude showed despising and ignorance toward God. He thought they must be idle and that the worship of God was unimportant and in vain (a lie of Satan), so he increased their workload tremendously. We see the proud, rebellious heart of Pharaoh, king of the strongest, most civilized nation on the earth. Rebellion and not knowing the God of Israel go side by side, for knowing God is the foundation of obedience to Him. At this time, Pharaoh ignored the God of the Hebrews, but later on he was forced to recognize Him by His mighty deeds.

When Moses was rebuked by the Israelite foremen, he must have felt hurt and possibly embarrassed. He could have been paralized and paranoid if he had listened to what the foremen said, and thus would have been unable to serve God the way he should. But Moses did not dwell on their cutting words. Though full of questions and doubts, he went immediately to the Lord in prayer. This is certainly the best thing for us to do as well, when we are troubled or in a difficult situation. But we should not have to wait until we have a problem to go the Lord. Even when things are going wonderfully, we should still thank Him and pray much. When Moses failed the first time on this mission, there might have been a great temptation to quit, but in going to the Lord he received new and greater strength.

Many times we tend to limit God, questioning Him and complaining when a problem arises. Discouragement may come because we cannot see beyond, but God can see the end, and He has everything in control. Sometimes He allows pressure so that greater salvation will follow.

The Lord's reply to Moses was full of grace and reassurance. He renewed to Him the promises of His covenant and commands and revealed His personal name *Jehovah*, giving Moses greater insight into its meaning, for now we see more the character attributes and the work of God. This will now be the name of their personal God, the God who cared and loved them when they were despised and enslaved in Egypt. They will not only know this by hearing, but will experience it by His power and love in redemption. Now His people have the right to depend on the name of God, the name which will save His people and lift them from distress to reveal His glory. The fuller revelation of God shows us the same in the name of Jesus Christ, the name above all names upon which we can depend.

Notice the six loving and encouraging promises that God gives the children of Israel: He will (1) bring them out in separation from the sinful life in Egypt and will (2) free them from their bondage. He will (3) redeem them. Here for the first time in the Bible we see the word *redeem*, referring to God's mighty act of salvation. Literally translated from Hebrew, it means to "untie", thus giving freedom, or to buy back from slavery. He will (4) take them as His people, for God chose Israel to be a light and an instrument in fulfilling His plan of salvation for the whole world which He loves. Likewise we as a Church, the people of God today, must not fail to be a light and an instrument in bringing the world to Him. God took them as His own to keep the promises He made to their forefathers (see Deuteronomy 7:7,8). God's love and care is seen, for even individuals are listed in the genealogy which serves to validate the leadership of Moses and Aaron over the children of Israel (6:14-27). Then God promised (5) to bring them into the land, which He will (6) give to them as an heritage or a possession. Therefore, God told Moses to tell Pharaoh "he must let the children of Israel go out of his land" (6:10). Now we see a broader request; they are to leave the land permanently and not just for three days. They must be out and free to enjoy the redemption of the Lord.

Isn't it the same for our salvation today? We must be away totally from worldly things if we are to enjoy the Lord's salvation to the fullest. Our salvation is accomplished by the work of God and not of our own strength, power or goodness, lest anyone should boast (Ephesians 2:8,9).

Prayer for today: *O Lord, according to Your promises, You hear us when we pray. Please give us greater wisdom and strength in order to serve You better.*

Read Exodus 7 & 8 *February 24*

Key Verse: Exodus 7:5 *"And the Egyptians shall know that I am the Lord, when I stretch out My hand on Egypt and bring out the children of Israel from among them."*

The Lord continued speaking with Moses in answering his complaints. The important thing is that the Lord told him the results of His miraculous signs and wonders in great judgments upon Egypt (because of their cruel slavery to the children of Israel and for killing the baby boys). Pharaoh's heart would continue to be hardened, but in the end the Egyptians would know that the Lord is God and He would bring out His host of people. With this encouragement, new boldness, and with the authority of God, Moses, at the age of 80 and Aaron at 83, went before Pharaoh in obedience to the Lord's command. Following the Lord's instructions to Moses, Aaron, when asked for a sign, threw down his rod which became a serpent. It is amazing that Pharaoh's magicians did the same, and they also could copy the first two plagues which were most likely "lying wonders" empowered by Satan (2 Thessalonians 2:9). However, the supremacy of God and the limitation of their power was seen when Aaron's serpent swallowed up theirs and in the fact that they were helpless to undo the plagues which God had brought upon the land. Whatever God does, Satan cannot undo.

Pharaoh still strengthened his will (hardened his heart) against God and was unyeilding to let the people go. There are three different Hebrew words used to describe the condition of Pharaoh's heart: "to make strong" (7:13,22; 8:19); "to make heavy, slow to move" (7:14; 8:15,32); and "to harden" (7:13). The hardening of Pharaoh's heart by God was done because Pharaoh had already, on his own, hardened his heart against God. God's purpose was to make Pharaoh repent, but when someone sets himself against God, even His mercies result in further hardening. Because of Pharaoh's proud, rebellious heart, God brought ten plagues on Egypt within a relatively short period of time, and the final one resulted in the Exodus (meaning "going out") of Israel. The plagues became progressively more severe and were directed against the gods of Egypt (12:12) to show that the God of the Hebrews is the One true God. The Nile was worshipped as a god and the frog was regarded as holy — a symbol of fertility and bounty. The plagues also served to show the Hebrews there was to be no other gods before Him.

After Moses warned Pharaoh, he had Aaron stretch out his rod and literally all the water of the Nile, and even water in jars, turned to actual blood. God was merciful, so this first plague lasted for only seven days. The second plague (frogs) was supernatural because they were tremendously increased. By asking Moses to intercede and make the frogs leave, Pharaoh confessed the existence and power of their God, but his heart remained hardened towards Him. True confession of God should be followed by the belief of the heart. God did according to Moses' request and, at a set time, the frogs miraculously died. But Pharaoh was not an honourable person and again he refused to let them go. The third plague, lice (better translated as a stinging gnat), came without warning and Pharaoh's magicians could not copy it. They confessed it was an act of God and may have intended their comment as a warning that Pharaoh should let the Hewbrews go. Still Pharaoh strengthened his will against God.

In the fourth plague, God made a distinction between the Israelites and the Egyptians. The Egyptians, who prided themselves on cleanliness, felt their land had been "corrupted" or ruined because of the flies. These were probably a biting kind of fly that may cause diseases. Pharaoh told them they could go and sacrifice but they were to remain in his land. This compromise was not acceptable. God demands total obedience. Moses wisely said that if they sacrificed "the abomination" (8:26), the Egyptians might kill them, for they considered some animals to be holy, such as the calf, and slaughtering them was forbidden. Then Pharaoh said they could go to the wilderness but not very far. Halfway obedience is not obedience at all. This is like the sly tricks of Satan, who tries to keep those following God still close to the bad influences of the world. To truly enjoy the redemption of the Lord, the redeemed people must be separate from the evil of the world (2 Cor. 6:17).

Prayer for today: *Mighty God, soften our hearts so that we may be sensitive, knowing and doing Your will always.*

Read Exodus 9 *February 25*

Key Verse: Exodus 9:16 *"But indeed for this purpose I have raised you up, that I may show My power in you, and that My name may be declared in all the earth."*

Moses continues untiringly before Pharaoh — "let My people go". Each plague was conditioned upon Pharaoh's stubborn refusal. The plagues crippled the greatest nation on earth, but before most of them there came a warning, and for those who feared the God of the Israelites there was relief from the effects of the plague. The fifth plague was a severe and fatal disease targeted against the sacred bull and cow. It hit all the livestock of the Egyptians who did not heed the warning and who had left their livestock out "in the field" (9:3). When the Bible reads "all" it must be a general term for "most", since later we see that those Egyptians who feared God and once again heeded the warning brought their livestock in from the field so that the plague of hail would not kill them (9:20,21). The Lord set a time when the plague would come and He once again made a distinction between the Egyptian's livestock and the Israelite's. All this, Moses related to Pharaoh beforehand, so he could see for himself that it was the power of their God. Indeed not one of the Israelite's livestock were killed or affected by this disease, yet Pharaoh continued to further harden his heart.

The sixth plague of boils came without warning as a sudden judgment upon the Egyptians and even their beasts. Pharaoh's magicians were no exception. Their powers could not cure the boils and they came under the judgment of God for resisting the truth (see 2 Timothy 3:8,9). Again we see the stubbornness and rebellion of Pharaoh which caused God to harden his heart.

Before the seventh plague God sent Moses to warn Pharaoh, saying, "Let my people go, so that they may worship Me, or this time I will send the full force of My plagues against you" (9:14, N.I.V). God told Moses to tell Pharaoh that He could have killed him and his people in order to free Israel, but God preserved Pharaoh's life so that he might experience Jehovah's mighty wonders and as a result the Name of God and His mighty deeds in judgment would be declared throughout the whole earth (9:15,16; The Apostle Paul quotes this verse in Romans 9:17 to express the sovereignty of God). It was God's desire that the whole world might know and believe in Him, not just one country. Later on in history, the nation of Israel missed part of their purpose as being a light for all nations. Today the believers in Jesus are to be lights to the world (Philippians 2:15). We see a similar picture foretold in the last days when the wrath of God will be poured on the earth, but rather than repent, they will curse God (Revélations 16:9,11,21). The seventh plague was a terrible hail and lightening storm which killed anything that was exposed, including plants and trees. It was against the gods Isis and Seth who were believed to be their protectors from such disasters.

There had never been anything like that in Egypt before or since that time. Once again, God gave a gracious warning of the coming danger (just as He does today) so that those who believe and fear Him might save their livestock and themselves by taking cover. Again Israel was completely spared. God also showed His mercy in the timing of the storm for, although it destroyed the barley and flax, it came too early to destroy the wheat, which was an important staple for them.

This plague brought Pharaoh to the point of confessing that he had sinned, but Moses, with the gifts of discernment and knowledge, knew that he was not really humble or sincere and his heart was still against God (9:30). Pharaoh was not sorry for his sin, he was merely sorry for the result of it. Moses set the time for when he would stop the storm, so they might again know it was the Lord's doing, for "the earth is the Lord's" (9:29). When Pharaoh saw the storm had stopped, he again hardened his heart as God had told Moses he would do.

Prayer for today: O God, grant us the grace to be genuinely sorry for our sin. Forgive us for the times when we're only sorry for the consequences of our sin.

Read Exodus 10 February 26

Key Verse: Exodus 10:9 *"And Moses said, 'We will go with our young and our old; with our sons and our daughters, with our flocks and our herds we will go, for we must hold a feast to the Lord.'"*

The Lord continued to harden the already hard heart of Pharaoh so that further and greater judgments would come upon Egypt and so that the Israelites could pass on from generation to generation the story of the great and mighty signs and wonders that

God, the One and only, did to the land which oppressed and enslaved them (10:2). Pharaoh was very proud and he exalted himself over the children of Israel (9:17) and now we hear from God Himself that he refused to humble himself before the Lord (10:3). The Lord will not share His glory with anyone. Pharaoh was like a god to his people, but he could never be this for the children of Israel. They knew better and this may have made him extremely jealous of a God who was unseen and yet who proved Himself to be almighty. Pharaoh was a sinner who thought he could challenge God. He was certainly proven wrong and he himself had to confess this.

Moses warned Pharaoh that the eighth plague of locusts would come the next day if he did not let his people go. Pharaoh's servants must have been aware of the damage locusts could cause and they were bold in speaking up to Pharaoh, perhaps trying to get him to reconsider, saying, "Do you not yet know that Egypt is destroyed?" Pharaoh must have known of the destruction thus far, but he was too proud, calloused, and insensitive to care about anyone but himself.

For the third time (10:11) Pharaoh tried to make Moses agree to a compromise (cf. 8:25,28), suggesting that only the men go out (leaving the children and women to ensure the men's return). No, this could not be accepted; the whole family must be together to worship the Lord and be included in the salvation of the Lord. Pharaoh, angered by Moses' answer, rudely has Aaron and himself "driven out" (10:11). Once again, Moses was refused his request and so came the east wind which blew for 24 hours, bringing from a distance with the current of the wind, the greatest locust plague the world has ever seen. Anything green that remained from the plague of hail was totally eaten up by the locusts (see Joel 1:4-12). Locusts are like an army, they keep advancing forward. In front of them is green, behind them is barren land. This plague was supernatural; the locusts came right when Moses predicted they would, there was a superabundance of them, and they stopped and were driven into the Red sea by a miraculous change of wind at the time when Moses prayed.

The plague of darkness came without warning, like the third and sixth plagues. When Moses obeyed God and stretched out his hands a miraculous thick darkness came suddenly upon the land where the Egyptians lived. Also miraculous was the fact that the land of Goshen (where the Israelites lived) had light, of what nature we are not told, but since the sun was darkened it may have been an unexplainable heavenly light. We always see that God uses people (even the weak and despised) as His instruments to accomplish His will. May the Lord use us as His instruments today to show forth the glory of the Lord. This plague lasting for three days, was a humiliation and a direct blow to the highest and most important god of the Egyptians, the sun god Re. To see him defeated meant his power was blotted out over Egypt, and the Israelite God was supreme.

With this, Pharaoh called Moses to try for the fourth time to get him to compromise by leaving behind all the livestock (10:24) as a guarantee of their return. How could they worship God without anything to sacrifice? No, there could be no compromise. God certainly requires all that we possess and Moses made this very clear to Pharaoh. Pharaoh had met his match with Moses, but Moses was to be the winner. When one is on God's side, he is the ultimate winner. Pharaoh, in a burst of anger, threatened that if he saw Moses' face again it would mean his death. Moses agreed that they would never see each other again. We read later that he too became angry, for Pharaoh had repeatedly refused the opportunities given him and now a more drastic and serious measure was to be taken.

Prayer for today: *O Lord, all that we have is Yours. Grant that we will worship You with our substance as well as our lives.*

Read Exodus 11 & 12   *February 27*

Key Verse: Exodus 12:13 *"Now the blood shall be a sign for you on the houses where you are. And when I see the blood, I will pass over you".*

Here we have recorded the greatest event in the history of Israel. After waiting patiently for Pharaoh to repent and let His people go, God, in His wrath, brought His most solemn and serious judgment on this rebellious nation. The last of the ten plagues, the death of the first born of both man and animal, was the climax of the whole ordeal with Pharaoh in which God ended with victory. Moses gave Pharaoh ample warning to let them go before the plague struck and again he told Pharaoh that God would make a distinction between Israel and Egypt. Moses became angered by Pharaoh's rebellion in his complete rejection of God and by what the consequences such action would have to be (11:8). Pharaoh's hardening his heart led to the destruction of Egypt and from that point it began to decline.

God gave Moses complete instructions on how to properly observe the Passover, and how they were to leave Egypt. Commemoration of this event marks the beginning of the Jewish religious year, the month of Aviv, in March or April, according to the moon. The Lord stressed to His people that this first feast, founded on God's deliverance through sacrifice, was a very important lasting ordinance (12:14,17,24,42) to be observed yearly by the whole family. Its significance was to be passed on from generation to generation (12:26,27). In the same way today, the foundation for a successful family life is spiritual success. Instructing our children about the Lord is the best teaching they will ever receive.

The Passover has great significance for us as well, for it typified our Lord Jesus Christ, the Lamb of God. The New Testament clearly states that Jesus the Messiah is our Passover (1Corinthians 5:7). The Passover lamb was to be without blemish (12:5). Jesus Christ was perfect, He was without sin (Hebrews 4:15; 1 John 3:5), and no fault could be found with Him (Luke 23:4), as such He was the ultimate sacrifice. The lamb's blood applied on the doorposts and lintel was evidence that those in the home were prepared and obedient. When the final judgment day of the Lord comes we, too, must be prepared and covered by the blood of Jesus. That was not only a night of destruction, it was also a night of salvation for those who believed. The book of Hebrews explains, "without the shedding of blood there is no remission [forgiveness]" (Hebrews 9:22). The precious blood of Christ was shed for our redemption and our deliverence from the sinfulness of this world. The blood of Jesus is made effective when the repentant sinner applies it to his soul by believing that Jesus, the Son of God, died, was buried, rose on the third day and lives today to forgive our sins and that by His blood we are cleansed from all unrighteousness (1 John 1:9). In the Old Testament ritual, the blood was sprinkled with the hyssop plant and this came to be a symbol of purification as on the Day of Atonement (Psalm 51:7; Hebrews 9:19-22).

Pharaoh heard the great cry as the Lord struck all the first born in the homes that were unprepared. Finally he agreed, without trying to make a compromise, that the children of Israel might go, every one and all the livestock too. Their Egyptian neighbours were glad to give articles of silver and gold (later to be used in the Tabernacle) as the Lord had commanded His people to ask of them (11:2) and, as He had fortold, they would not go out empty handed (3:21,22). What they received was due payment for all the many years of slave labour that Israel had suffered in Egypt. A conservative estimate of about 2 million people left Egypt that day, fulfilling the prophesies God had given to their forefathers. They left 430 years from the same day that Jacob entered with his 75 family members (Acts 7:14). Their increase was tremendous, because the blessing of the Lord was upon them (Exodus 1:7). We see the grace of God in permitting "a mixed multitude"

(12:38) to leave with the Israelites. They must have desired to follow the Lord and His leading. The people of Israel were to be the mediators for the other nations, so that through them others might come to believe in God. We see they were never meant to be alone, but to welcome strangers (Isaiah 56:3-8). Even in the Old Testament the door was open for all who wanted to participate in the redemption of the Lord.

Prayer for today: *God of Moses and of the people of Israel, we pray the Blood of Your sacrifical Lamb, our Lord Jesus, to be over us as our protection now and forever.*

Read Exodus 13 *February 28*

Key Verse: Exodus 13:2 *"Sanctify to Me all the firstborn, whatever opens the womb among the children of Israel, both of man and animal; it is Mine."*

After the Lord struck down all the first born of Egypt and redeemed the first born of the Israelites (those covered by the blood of the sacrificial lamb), He asked that they be sanctified unto Him, meaning they were to be consecrated, or set apart for His service. The Israelites were to do this as a constant reminder and also as an act of gratitude to God for having had their first born preserved by Him in His act of grace. God is speaking to a people redeemed by the blood, so they all must be set apart for Him; set apart from sin and the world to be dedicated to the Lord and to enjoy the life of redemption by fellowship with Him. God has called us, as believers in the Lord Jesus and the "church of the first born" (Hebrews 12:23) to a life with a deeper relationship with Him. He calls us to be sanctified and separated from the sin of the world to live a more consecrated and holy life which is pleasing to Him.

The unleavened bread was to also serve as a reminder of the haste in which they left Egypt (12:34), for they did not have time to let the yeast work so the bread would rise. In the Bible yeast came to be a symbol for sin, and a corrupting influence (Matthew 13:33;16:6; 1 Cor. 5:6-8) which must be removed from one's life to see the deliverance of the Lord accomplished.

The Lord commanded them to teach their children from generation to generation so that His mighty hand in delivering them would always be remembered even as a sign on the hand and a memorial (or a reminder) on the forehead (13:9). The religious orthodox Jews of today have taken this part of the verse literally and so often in prayer they actually tie segments of the Law in little boxes around their hand and on their forehead, however, these are figurative expressions meaning to keep it in remembrance, just as the figurative expression in the same verse, "the Lord's law may be in your mouth" means to always keep it in conversation.

The Lord not only saved them, but also stayed with them. His presence was among them to guide and protect on their journey by the pillar of cloud in the day. In the night this same pillar was seen as fire, expressing His kindness and care toward them. In His wisdom and understanding, God led them in the way of the wilderness, rather than through the hostile territory of the Philistines which was the closer and more direct way to Canaan. When the people were ready, and all in God's good timing, they would enter the land of Canaan as He promised them. However it was not until after 40 years of wandering in the wilderness that they were finally ready to enter their Promised Land. After this time of testing and being humbled, they learned discipline, patience in hardships, and to follow God's commandments and trust in Him (see Deuteronomy 8:2-4). The Lord never forsook them, and since He was with them no power could stand against them.

We see again that this story is linked with Genesis, when Moses took Joseph's bones in fulfillment of his request given about 350 years before when he prophesied that God would surely come and help them out of Egypt (Genesis 50:24,25). The Passover was in the plan of God and the means in which He delivered them out of bondage. Today we continue to see that the Lord is faithful in delivering us from sin, in keeping His promises and in taking care of His people, the Church.

Prayer for today: *O Lord, as You were with Israel, be with us. We need You as our cloud by day and pillar of fire by night. Lead and guide in Your way.*

MARCH

*A view from the inside of the Garden Tomb,
believed to be the site of Jesus' burial and resurrection.*

Key Verse: Exodus 14:13 *"Do not be afraid. Stand still, and see the salvation of the Lord, which He will accomplish for you today..."*.

After the Israelites had traveled for three days, Pharaoh heard they had fled rather than making a pilgrimage to offer sacrifices. He realized the great loss and the great value of those slaves and wanted them back. Moses, following the instructions of the Lord, had led the people to a seemingly defenceless position, with the sea behind them and the wilderness in front. This enticed Pharaoh to recapture them, but his plan was but a part of God's larger plan, for He had one final lesson to teach Egypt. God hardens Pharaoh's heart so that He may bring further judgment upon him and his army, to show them once again, His great power that they might know Him as greater than Pharaoh and any of their gods.

The Lord had a lesson for the Israelites to learn as well. In this event they saw God as the all-powerful Holy judge of the ungodly so they might grow in the fear of Him. They also saw Him as their protector; this gave them the added faith they needed for their journey since they would come against great odds. At this point, however, the people were terrified and as slaves they would have been without weapons, so they complained to Moses. This the psalmist called rebellion against God (Psalm 106:7). Humanly speaking they were faced with certain recapture and possibly many would be killed. They still had to learn to trust in God. Moses spoke boldly to them with great faith in Almighty God that the battle was His. Today, when we come up against the enemy, we can still be sure that our God will fight for us and be victorious!

The Lord put His pillar between the Egyptians and the Israelites. He made darkness for the enemy, but on His children's side He gave them light to see their way across the sea. The pillar not only gave them supernatural divine protection, but it concealed their movements from the Egyptians. They did not cross at a shallow swampy area as some liberal critics propose, but walked across on the dried sea bottom. The parting was not caused by a tide as some say in trying to explain away the supernatural, because there were walls of water on **both** sides of them. It was truly a miraculous event from God. When Moses held out his rod, God sent the east wind to part the water and dry the sea bed.

Once all the Israelites were across safely, Moses used the same motion and God let the walls of water fall in on the Egyptians. As they saw it was the hand of God and tried to flee, He confused them and sent them into a panic. "He took off their chariot wheels". This might have been because God, who had miraculously kept the sea bottom dry for the Israelites to cross, allowed it to become muddy and soft again, causing the wheels to get stuck and fall off. We read that not one of the Israelites' enemies were left; this means that Pharaoh as well, their greatest enemy, must have died (14:28; Psalm 106:11). The bodies of many Egyptian soldiers were swept ashore, no doubt supplying Israel with a great quantity of weapons which they would need at a later time.

The Lord's love, care and guidance of His people is beautifully described in Isaiah 63:12. "Who led them by the right hand of Moses, with His glorious arm, dividing the water before them to make for Himself an everlasting name." The next two verses continue to express the care and concern of the Lord who led them so they would not even stumble. He gave them peace and rest by His Spirit and in His leading made for Himself a glorious name. Indeed, the news of this miraculous act of God reached and alarmed the surrounding nations who came to fear the God of the Israelites (15:14-16).

Prayer for today: *Great miraculous God, we wait for Your supernatural acts. Only You can do those necessary acts which are humanly impossible.*

Read Exodus 15   *March 2*

Key Verse: *"You in Your mercy have led forth*
The people whom You have redeemed;
You have guided them in Your strength
To Your holy habitation." (Exodus 15:13)

What a beautiful song of praise unto the Lord! It is a victory song of deliverance. God's character and mighty deeds are lifted up in thanksgiving. After seeing their miraculous salvation by His hand in crossing the sea, the Lord's triumph over the proud Pharaoh and the destruction of their enemies, the children of Israel had good reason to worship the Lord with great joy. They must have stood in awe and reverence of His Holiness and power. God alone received all the glory, for the people acknowledged their helplessness without Him.

Moses' song is a beautiful example of Hebrew poetry in which each phrase or line is repeated in similar words in the next line, or sometimes two thoughts are contrasted. "I will praise Him" and "I will exalt Him" is a typical example from verse two. Most of this poem is in the same fashion of synonymous parallel structure.

94

Verse 8 clearly states that the waters parted, heaped up, and the bottom was "congealed" (i.e. *became firm*), caused by the supernatural power of God, and not by some natural phenomenon. The Lord is described as a warrior who, in His mercy and loving kindness, fought the battle for His children and was triumphant over all the Egyptian gods and Pharaoh. It is also a song of prophecy. The Lord will lead them, because of His mercy, to His holy habitation (15:13). This is Mount Sinai or Horeb, where God appeared to Moses in the burning bush and where He would once again appear to give the ten commandments. The surrounding nations of Palestina (the Philistines), Edom (descendants of Esau), and Moab (from Lot, Gen. 19:36-37) will fear God's power as His people whom He has "purchased" (redeemed, brought back from slavery) pass through their territory (15:16). The Lord will lead them and "plant" (firmly establish) them in the mountain of His inheritance which is Mount Moriah in Jerusalem, the sight of the future Temple (15:17). The song ends on a glorious note expressing God's eternal kingship (15:18). We need to understand that God has always and will always continue to be in control.

After Moses' song, his sister Miriam joyfully joined in leading the women in song and dance unto the Lord. It seems the first verse of the song was repeated as the chorus (15:1, 21), and she sang in answer to the men. She was called a prophetess because the Lord used her in a leadership capacity (Micah 6:4).

God continued to lead Israel to a place of testing: to the bitter waters of Marah (meaning *bitter*). The people complained against Moses rather than trusting in God. Moses prayed and the Lord immediately gave him instructions. Moses was a good example: it is better to pray rather than complain. God changed the natural element into the supernatural (cf. John 9:6). The bitter water was not replaced, but became sweet, not because of a certain quality of the tree, but by the power of God. This demonstrated God's care and love for His people and would help them to develop character.

God promised them that if they were obedient to Him, they would not be touched with the diseases that struck the Egyptians. Along with this promise He gave a new revelation of Himself as "Jehovah Rapheh", the Lord who heals. God's people can depend upon Him for their healing just as He healed the bitter water.

Following this short trial came a longer period of rest at Elim, an oasis in the wilderness, a perfect place to set up camp. God's loving kindness is abundant! He will always provide the needs of His children!

Read Exodus 16 *March 3*

Key Verse: Exodus 16:15-16 *"...This is the bread which the Lord has given you to eat...Let every man gather it according to each one's need".*

Once again the Lord preserved the children of Israel: this time from hunger. About one month after leaving Egypt, food was scarce. Upon remembering the good food they enjoyed in Egypt, they began to complain to Moses who rebuked them for they were really complaining against God. It is true that when believers complain and are discontent, they are actually complaining against God, for He has a purpose and is in control of all things. The Bible teaches that whatever our state, we are to be content, for Jesus said, "I will never leave you nor forsake you" (Hebrews 13:5). God is kind and compassionate, and fully understands human weakness. Rather than rebuking the Israelites, He began to test and teach them to daily trust and depend on Him. To prepare them for the miracle, there was the unmistakeable evidence of the Lord's presence in the cloud which probably had an unusual shining radiance to show them the importance of what was to be said.

God always gives the best to His children, not only for necessity, but for delight as well. Each morning He gave them their new staple of manna, a special food from heaven, and each evening He gave them fowl in abundance. These miraculous provisions not only gave them sustenance, but, more importantly, taught His faithfullness, goodness, and constant divine presence among them. Certain instructions were to be followed serving to test their obedience. However, when they gathered manna on the Sabbath the Lord rebuked them. He desired obedience from His children, just as He expects it from believers today. He said, "How long do you refuse to keep My commandments and My laws?" (16:28). This shows that the Sabbath was already known. It had been instituted by God after His work of creation (Genesis 2:2-3); however, previous to that time it had not been observed in any special way.

God gave the Sabbath to His redeemed people as a gift (16:29): a day they needed to be refreshed, both physically and spiritually, before the work week began. Believers today, as well, need to dedicate this special day to the Lord in worship and meditation on Him.

The manna (meaning, "what is it?") was not a natural phenomenon; it came supernaturally from God. In the Middle East there is a white substance that is found on a particular kind of tree. Some Bible commentators, trying to explain away the supernatural have said this is the same as the manna of the Bible. However the differences far outweigh any similarities. Like the manna of the Bible this white substance comes in the early morning, melts in the hot sun and has a sweet flavour, however it is seasonal, found only in the summer. The manna of the Bible was gathered all year round for 40 years until, just as suddenly as it had appeared, it miraculously stopped when the Israelites entered Canaan. It was found everywhere on the ground, not just on certain trees. The white substance that some Beduoins gather today can only be boiled down to make a sweet syrup; it cannot be ground or baked into bread or cakes as the Israelites had done, as well as boiling it (16:23).

Clearly, the manna was a divine and miraculous provision from God. Another miracle was that if the manna was kept overnight, except on the Sabbath, it would spoil. The only reason it did not spoil on the morning of the Sabbath was that it was sanctified by God's word. Six nights out of seven the people went to bed without any of their staple food in the house. They had to learn contentment and trust God to supply in the morning.

In the Bible, manna is a symbol of three heavenly gifts from God which are our spiritual support and comfort while we are in the wilderness of this world: (1) Jesus, the most precious gift from God, regarded manna as a shadow of Himself, the true Bread of life from heaven (John 6:31-35). Anyone coming to Him will be fully satisfied. (2) The Word of God, by which our souls are nourished, is pictured in the manna (see Matthew 4:4; Deuteronomy 8:3). And (3) for those who overcome, the reward and comforts of the Spirit are "hidden manna" (Revelation 2:17).

Prayer for today: Our Lord, You have made daily provision for us. Thank You for the bread of Life, our Lord Jesus. Help us to partake of Him, by faith daily through prayer and reading His Word.

Read Exodus 17 *March 4*

Key Verse: Exodus 17:6 *"Behold, I will stand before you there on the rock in Horeb; and you shall strike the rock, and water will come out of it, that the people may drink."*

As soon as the children of Israel felt thirsty, they began to complain once again. Had they forgotten so soon the provision of the Lord with the meat and manna? When believers find they are in a dark place they tend to forget the light of yesterday; however they must learn that this Light, God's presence, never abandons them. Israel failed on this test of faith. Their hearts were not right before the Lord; it seemed they loved Him when everything went well, but when problems arose they forgot the love and trust they should have for God and complained against Him.

There is a lesson for believers not to worry about anything (Matthew 6:33) but to love, worship, and praise God in all circumstances. Like Moses, when we face a problem, we need to cry out to the Lord in prayer (17:4) for He hears and is faithful to give us the strength to overcome. The trials we face today often lead to spiritual growth. In the same way, the difficulties Israel had were tests so God could teach them trust, obedience, and love for Him before they would be spiritually mature enough to enter Canaan (Deut. 8:2-5).

In God's gracious and miraculous provision of water, He met their evil doing with His goodness, their complaints with His great love. The elders, as eye witnesses, told their tribes of the miraculous flow of water from the solid rock, thus all the Israelites would clearly know that the water was provided directly from God, and with Him nothing was impossible.

In the New Testament writings of the Apostle Paul, we learn that just as the manna typified Jesus, so also do the water and the Rock which he said to be "spiritual" (1 Corinthians 10:4). The water flowed out in abundance as do the blessings of the Lord and living water flow out from Jesus Christ, the Source of life eternal (John 4:14). And Jesus has said that whoever believes in Him will receive by His Spirit, rivers of living water flowing out of His heart (John 7:38,39). The rock which was struck represents Jesus, whose life-giving blood was shed for us that we might see His salvation. Jesus is truly our Rock; He is our refuge and strength on whom we can always depend.

After the miraculous provision of the water, Israel was forced for the first time to engage in battle. This was the first attempt of interference with their journey to Canaan. Amalek represents evil which tries to prevent the work of God, but with intercessory prayer the enemy is defeated and the Lord is the victor. The Amalekites (descendants of Esau; their name meaning giants) were mighty men of war who did not fear God and, as we are told later, ruthlessly attacked the weak from the rear. Their unrighteous behavior caused them to be considered an abomination to the Lord and their judgment was total destruction (Deuteronomy 25:16-19; Exodus 17:14).

In verse nine we have the first mention of Joshua, whom Moses gave responsibility to choose men to fight. Moses must have taken note of Joshua's leadership capabilites and, in the providence of God, selected him to lead the people in battle. Joshua later became their leader.

In the previous encounter with their enemy, the Lord had fought **for** His people (Exodus 14:14); now we see here that the Lord fights **through** His people. This is exactly illustrated in the New Testament: the first battle was won on the cross by Jesus Christ alone as He crushed the enemy and was victorious over death so that we may enjoy the peace of His salvation. The second battle was, and still is, the war of the Holy Spirit through us — a continuous battle against the flesh, but we have assurance that the victory is ours and with our faith we can overcome the world (1 John 5:4,5).

Prayer is essential for victory. As we see, Moses held up his hands as an act of intercessory prayer and dependance upon God, showing all the people the reality of this dependance. With the help of his supporters, Aaron and Hur, the battle was won. God's leaders (our pastors) need to be held up in prayer and encouraged so they may remain strong, for they are engaged in spiritual warfare with our enemy, Satan. When we constantly and fervently hold them up, and ourselves, in prayer, we will see the victory!

Prayer for today: *Dear Lord, You are our Rock, smitten on the Cross. We partake of You, Living Water, and our thirst is quenched.*

Read Exodus 18   March 5

Key Verse: Exodus 18:19 *"Listen to my voice; I will give you counsel, and God will be with you: Stand before God for the people, so that you may bring the difficulties to God."*

The news of Israel's triumph over the Egyptians spread to the surrounding nations. Jethro, Moses' father-in-law in Midian, heard of it and came to hear more details and to reunite Moses with his wife and two sons after being apart for several months. It seems Moses had sent them back after the circumcision of his son (Exodus 4:24-26) for he may have sensed danger ahead and felt they may have been a hindrance to his mission.

Moses, though a great prophet and leader, humbly bowed before his father-in-law for whom he showed much respect. Jethro, a descendant of Abraham through Katurah (Gen. 25:1-2), was a godly man, and although a Gentile he worshipped the One true and living God. For forty years, Moses had lived under his godly influence. He rejoiced with Moses upon hearing of all that happened in Egypt and the goodness of God in delivering Israel. When we see people come to experience the Lord's salvation and when other believers tell of God's goodness, we should give praise to God and rejoice with them. Sharing God's goodness together is pleasing to the Lord. It helps to edify and encourage one another, like Jethro, whose faith was strengthened when Moses talked with him of God's goodness (18:11). It is also important to share our salvation with unbelievers, for in hearing, they too may come to believe.

Since the priesthood of Israel had not yet been established, Jethro, a Gentile priest in Midian, led and possibly instigated the offering of a sacrifice in worship to the Lord. Then, along with Moses, Aaron and the elders, he ate of the "bread", which we may assume was manna. In eating it, Jethro could literally "taste and see that the Lord is good" (Psalm 34:8). He, as a Gentile along with the "mixed multitude" (12:38), was welcomed to share in the blessings of the Lord which are available to everyone who will come unto Him. Jethro shared this blessed bread with them "before God" (18:12) and as such we know it was a sanctified, God-centred feast. Fellowship around the table gives opportunity for glorifying God as we centre our conversation on Him and "all His wondrous works" (Psalm 105:2). Of course, all we do should glorify God, not just because His eye is always on us, but out of love for Him and a desire to please Him.

God used Jethro to give very important and wise advice to Moses. Being a godly man, he conditioned his suggestion: "if...God so commands you" (18:23). Nothing should be done out of the will of God. It may be assumed that Moses inquired of the Lord and had the go-ahead to act upon the advise of Jethro. The wise leader is one who will take counsel from other spiritually mature elders. It was common among the ancient semitic tribes that the leader also be the judge (cf. 1 Samuel 7:15-17), but for Moses it was clear that it was too exhausting for him alone to carry this great responsibility. Because Moses was the spiritual leader, Jethro suggested he spend his time more in prayer (18:19 — key verse) for the wisdom needed to lead such a people. With the delegation of qualified, trained men to act as judges, Moses was relieved for greater and more essential duties. Some pastors and other church leaders today need to follow Moses' example.

Moses perfected an organized system of higher and lower courts which was used by Israel for centuries to come. Moses himself chose the judges, for the children of Israel had proven they were unfit to decide for themselves. The magistrates were required to first come under the training of Moses that they might know the statutes and laws of God and walk upright before Him (18:20). Secondly, their personal qualifications had to meet a certain standard: they were to be "able men", wise, intelligent, having the fear of God, and only those who loved truth and hated covetousness. This was necessary, for justice is often corrupted when those in authority take bribes.

Prayer for today: *Thank You for using Jethro, a non Israelite, to show Your love for all people. Reveal Yourself, O God, all over the world, to all people.*

Read Exodus 19   *March 6*

Key Verse: Exodus 19:5 *"If you will indeed obey My voice and keep My covenant, then you shall be a special treasure to Me above all people".*

The multitude of Israelite slaves that left Egypt were now a free people becoming an organized nation. Moses led them by the guidance of God to Mount Sinai which, it seems, is one very high peak of a mountain range called Horeb. They were traveling alongside this range (17:6), which they considered "the mountain [range] of God" (18:5), until they reached their destination — the very place where Moses saw the burning bush (3:1,2) and was promised a "sign" (3:12). Moses alone went up to commune with God while the people camped in the territory below.

While Moses was on the mountain, God revealed His intention concerning the redeemed nation of Israel. God, as an act of grace and out of His own goodwill, had decided to allow them the privilege of entering into a covenant relationship with Him. In giving the covenant, the Lord reminded them of their swift redemption from Egypt and the grace He had extended to them. He carried them as though on "eagles' wings" (19:4), showing them His great care, protection and compassion. He was the maker of the covenant; it was not the people's idea, for they did not show interest in spiritual things. It was not imposed on them, but rather, out of their own free will, they were to respond to God. It is the same today; God does not make us believe in Him, rather He allows us the freedom to choose. Those that choose Him and enter into the New Covenant relationship under Jesus Christ truly enjoy the redemption He provides.

The covenant God laid before them was conditional: "**if** you will indeed obey My voice...**then** you shall be a special treasure...a kingdom of priests and a holy nation" (19:5,6). As such, they were to be mediators between God and man, called to tell the nations of the earth about the knowledge and salvation of God, but to have this honour, they were to be obedient to Him and keep His covenant. It was God's intention that all Israel be priests, but they later proved themselves unworthy. Therefore He chose only the tribe of Levi to be priests, for they did not fall into sin by worshipping the golden calf like the other Israelites (Ex. 32:26).

We are living today in the New Covenant era established by the perfect sacrifice of the Lord Jesus Christ with the blood He shed for us on the cross. In Titus 2:14 we read: "[Jesus Christ] who gave Himself for us, that He might redeem us from every lawless deed and purify for Himself **His own special people.**" The whole body of believers today are the people of God, His chosen people (Ephesians 1:4-6) and in Jesus every believer is a priest (Revelation 1:6); "a royal priesthood, a holy nation, His own special people, that you may proclaim the praises of Him who called you out of darkness into His marvelous light" (1 Peter 2:9).

After Moses told the people all that God had said, they were quick to answer "yes" in agreement to obey Him (19:8), like pledging allegiance to a King. Perhaps they did not fully understand the significance of the vow they made before God, nor of how unable they were to keep it. Often people make rash promises which they are unable to keep, but this was more than just a promise, it was a vow, an oath before God, therefore it was a serious matter which obliged them to keep the covenant in obeying God. Decisions to follow God are not to be taken lightly. It is serious and important; the best decision a person will ever make.

The awesome and terrifying manifestation of the Lord's presence on Mount Sinai was the fulfillment of the "sign" that God promised Moses (3:12). This must have given him great encouragement, but at the same time we read in Hebrews that he, as well as all the people were trembling with fear (Hebrews 12:21). Before the heavenly trumpet blasts and the Lord's voice was heard, the people had to be sanctified. They washed their clothes and abstained from relationships with their spouse as a symbol of purification. This dramatic, supernatural display showed clearly the holiness of God and His separation in holiness. May we "serve God acceptably with reverence and godly fear. For our God is a consuming fire" (Hebrew 12:28,29).

Read Exodus 20 — *March 7*

Key Verse: Exodus 20: 6a *"...But showing mercy to thousands, to those who love Me and keep My commandments."*

The Ten commandents in Exodus 20 are the heart of the Old Testament. They are very important and unique for they were spoken with the audible voice of God; they were written down with the finger of God, and He ordered that they be kept in the Ark of the Covenant for the Israelites to keep as a remembrance. Moses recorded them in his writings so all generations would remember, teach and follow God's commandments. They are the moral law which deals with our everyday life. They are the basis for ethics and in most cases for legislation today. If they were followed completely we would be living in a perfect society.

These commandments of God were given to Israel in the context of the covenant into which which they, as a redeemed people, had agreed to enter. God had given them the specific principles on which the covenant is based, expressing His authority as He said, "I am the Lord your God". He declared His sovereignty, oneness, and that He is their personal God who redeemed them. This was the foundation of the commandments which fall into two sections: (1) the first four deal with man's conduct and duty toward God; (2) the next six deal with man's conduct and duty toward fellow man.

Most of the commandments are given in the negative form of "thou shalt not", because God knows the evil intent of mankind's heart. The most distinctive feature of these principles is seen in the first two commandments: there is to be no other god, nor is there to be made any image of a god. The Israelites must have been influenced by the polytheism (worship of many gods) in Egypt, for the Lord gave these commandments first (20:3,4) then He re-emphasized them again to Moses (20:23), knowing their weakness. Soon afterwards, they made the image of the golden calf (Exodus 32:4). In these first two, as well as the next two commandments, the reverence of God is emphasized. This forms the basis for all the others. Jesus considered it the basic quality of man's approach to God as expressed in the first sentence of the Lord's prayer: "Hallowed be Thy Name". It is surprising that even believers in ordinary conversation use the Name of God in a light and trivial way, for anything short of using the Lord God's name in worship, glory and honour is using it in vain (20:7).

Also in honour and reverence to the Lord, the seventh day was to be a sabbath (cessation from work) unto Him. In the New Covenant, the sabbath on the seventh day (Saturday) is not set forth as binding, however the general principle behind this command is still relevant to us: having one day of rest out of seven, set aside for worshipping God. The early church naturally chose the first day of the week (Sunday) since it was Christ's resurrection day.

The second section begins with the only commandment that is given with a promise: if you honour your parents, you will have a long life (20:12). Disrespect for parents, is the beginning of the destruction of the home, so keeping this commandment is very important. A healthy and stable home life often leads to stability in all areas of life. In the sixth commandment, the sanctity of human life is upheld, since we are made in the image of God. This commandment against murder is sometimes used in opposition to capital punishment which is permissable in the Bible as a punishment for crime (Exodus 21:12; Romans 13:4). The meaning of the Hebrew word used for murder is premeditated killing of another human with evil intent. This commandment is applicable to whatever degrades and deprives a living human being from a full and rich life that God wills he should have. The unneccessary killing of unborn human life in abortion is definitely murder for it is degrading to humanity and takes away the baby's right to a life God has given.

The seventh commandment is directed to protect the sanctity of marriage, but Jesus expanded it to include all sexual immorality, both in thought as well as in deed (Matthew 5:27,28). Jesus, in reaffirming the ten commandments explained them all in a condensed form: love of God sums up the first four commandments, and love to man sum up the last six commandments (Matthew 22:37-40). The most inward of the ten is the last, against covetousness, which is not an external act but a hidden mental state leading to nearly every sin against a neighbour. It was essentially the sin of Adam and Eve in desiring that which was against the will of God. Our minds must be daily renewed by the Spirit of God to only desire that which is right and in keeping with His will.

The dramatic way in which God gave His commandments was so the Israelites would have a reverence, respect and a healthy fear of their Holy God that they might not sin. They were fearful of approaching God directly, so from then on a less direct way was employed; through Moses and through the altar and sacrfice. Today, believers go to God through Jesus Christ, our mediator, the One who intercedes on our behalf and to whom all the Old Testament sacrifices pointed.

The key to obeying the law of God comes from loving Him (see key verse). This is the origin of true righteousness, for without love for God, observance of the Law is of no avail. With mankind's fallen condition, we are unable to keep the commandments of God to perfection; but even if one could, it would not lead to salvation. Only love and faith in Jesus Christ, God's only begotten Son, brings salvation, then, once redeemed and in the new covenant relationship with Him, it is our obligation to obey His commands. God is merciful, and in His grace has sent us His Holy Spirit to give us strength, and when we do fall short and sincerely repent, we have the blessed assurance that He will forgive (1 John 1:9).

Prayer for today: Lord God, Your punishment for breaking Your law is death. Thank You Father, that Your Son Jesus, who always kept Your law, died for Me so that You could forgive Me.

Read Exodus 21 & 22　　*March 8*

Key Verse: Exodus 22:31a *"And you shall be holy men to Me".*

After the Lord had given the moral law it was expounded upon by the civil law to make it applicable to the Israelites' everyday life. This was intended to produce a peaceful, well-working, and holy society. The God given original law code was for Israel to have strict guidelines to follow and thereby maintain a high level of morality (to promote righteousness before God) within their society; a witness to the surrounding nations that they were the people of God.

Slavery was an integral institution throughout the whole world at that time. However, slavery among the Israelites showed a marked distinction; unlike the other nations, they gave their rights to their slaves. Women also were given rights and lifted up to a higher standing by these rulings. A man in poverty might be forced to sell his daughter into servanthood, but the laws assured him that she would be taken care of and her rights were strictly regarded.

In general, the rulings stressed the sanctity of human life. In most cases, capital punishment was carried out on whoever took a life. If one caused an accidental death, God provided a place of refuge so no revenge could be taken (21:13; cf. Numbers 35:6). God also provided rights and protection for unborn babies. If one caused injury to a pregnant woman and she miscarried, then that person must pay the penalty of death, "life for life" (21:22,23). This teaches that abortion was rightly a capital offense!

The penalties may seem harsh to us, but in that ancient culture there were no law enforcement officers or prisons, nor the fuller, final and complete revelation of God in Jesus Christ, our example. For them to understand the seriousness of a crime, the punishment must be just as serious. Severe punishments served as the only way to curb wrong behaviour. In this cultural context the laws were very thorough, fair and just. If the laws were followed, this expressed righteous behaviour before God. He, however, knows the heart, and knows if acts are done out of a pure motive which is real righteousness.

The laws express man's responsibility toward his fellowman to whom he must show respect. If anyone's rights were violated there must be restitution and recompense. Guilt by carelessness which causes harm to another, even if it be his animal, is still punishable. To do wrong to a neighbour is to sin against God. The seduction we read of here is concerning the loss of value because of the dowry (the moral crime is dealt with in Deuteronomy 22:22-29). The sin of witchcraft within the covenant people was punishable by death, as was the unspeakable sin of beastiality. Anyone found sacrificing unto any other god but the Lord was also condemned; these three sins were practiced in the heathen religions of surrounding nations, and Israel was to take no part in them.

Humanitarian laws were also enforced. God's care and protection of the foreigner, needy widow and ophan among Israel are consistently expressed throughout Scripture (cf. James 1:27). He hears the cry of those in need, and if they are mistreated, His wrath is stirred up (22:21-24; cf. Deut. 10: 18,19). Also, in care and protection of the poor among the covenant people, those who lent money to them were warned against making their burdens heavier by charging interest, but were instead instructed to do it out of the goodness of their heart; as well as returning a pledge of their cloak which they would use as a covering on the cold nights. All people must be treated with dignity and respect.

The first fruits and livestock were to be the Lord's, and the first born males were to be dedicated to Him as priests (22:29; cf. Exodus 13:2). All the terms of the covenant stressed the Israelites' responsibility and reverence to the Lord, not only in what they did, but in abstaining from what He forbade.

The fact that these laws deal with matters of immorality indicate the sinful condition of the Israelites, which the Apostle Paul says the Law could not overcome (Romans 8:3). But through God's own first born Son, "the righteous requirement of the law might be fulfilled in us who do not walk according to the flesh but according to the Spirit". (Romans 8:4) This then leads to "life and peace" (Romans 8:6) and a holy and righteous walk before God.

Prayer for today: *O Holy God, You've not only made provision for our forgiveness, You've written Your laws upon our hearts. Help us to surrender daily in obedience to You.*

Read Exodus 23 & 24   *March 9*

Key Verse: Exodus 24:8 *"Behold, the blood of the covenant which the Lord has made with you according to all these words."*

Now that the Israelites were given many good civil laws, care must be taken that they be carried out honestly and justly. Justice and judgment must not be perverted by falsehood, mob pressure or, any form of bias. A principle that Jesus taught was also taught here in the Old Covenant (23:4,5): "do good to those who hate you" (Matthew 5:44; cf. Proverbs 25:21,22; Romans 12:20), and there is the idea of the golden rule — do unto others as you would have them do unto you (Matthew 7:12). These are contrary to the attitude of the world and express a godliness and separation which is pleasing to God. If the Israelites followed these rules, they would be different from the surrounding heathen nations. Our actions and attitudes are in themselves a witness to others of the love of God in our hearts.

The celebrations of the sabbaths and feasts were not only duties of the covenant people, but were privileges for their enjoyment. They were the focal points of the Israelite social life. The sabbatical year served to provide for the poor, and, in the wisdom of God, it provided a time for the soil to be replenished. The observance of the sabbath day, along with being a religious observance, is here presented as humanitarian as it provided a time for all to be refreshed. As God doubled the manna on the sixth day, so they were to trust Him to provide an abundance in the sixth year so that in the seventh year of untoiled soil they would not go hungry.

The feasts were to serve as a remembrance of their redemption (by eating only unleavened bread) and of God's continual blessings and provision. He is the giver and source of all good things and the feasts gave the Israelites opportunity to show their appreciation by bringing Him gifts (23:15,17). The Canaanites had the superstitious religious rite of boiling a young goat in its mother's milk to bring a good harvest. The Israelites were to learn that harvest came as a blessing from the Lord and He was to receive the glory for it. God constantly reminded them not to become involved in heathen practices (23: 24, 32, 33). We must take care not to be influenced by the superstitions of the world and to remain separate from things which displease God.

The covenant concludes with promises and warnings. The angel that God set before Israel was surely a preincarnate manifestation of Jesus Christ. God said of Him, "My name is in Him", meaning God revealed Himself through Him. He dwelt among God's people, and now He who became flesh dwells among us (John 1:14). He never leaves, but rather leads His redeemed believers through difficulties in wilderness places and through enemy territory to the promised inheritance where He has prepared a place for His spiritual Israel (John 14:2). In God's wisdom and timing, He would gradually cause the inhabitants of the land to leave (23:28, could be a plague of literal hornets, or the sting of fear) so the Israelities could grow in number and fully occupy the Promised Land.

God called Moses, all the elders, Aaron and his two oldest sons to come before Him on Mount Sinai, but Moses alone went up closer to hear from Him further instructions and to write them down (attests to the Mosaic authorship, 24:4). All the people agreed to obey the rulings of the covenant. Sacrifice was necessary before the close relationship with God was possible, since mankind's sinful condition forfeits the favour of God. The blood that was sprinkled upon the altar signified that their lives, which had already been redeemed, were now dedicated and given to their Lord as a living sacrifice in a close and binding communion. The sprinkling of blood on the people and, most likely, on the 12 pillars (representing the 12 tribes) was done as a sign of God's acceptance and favour. Thus the covenant was ratified through blood.

In the same manner, Jesus Christ, the Mediator of the New Covenant, offered up Himself as a sacrifice on the cross and His shed blood was sprinkled on the altar in intercession on our behalf (Hebrews 9:12) and sprinkled on His Church, the body of believers, to be made acceptable before God. Jesus seemed to allude to this portion of scripture (24:8) in His words at the Last Supper: "This cup is the new covenant in My blood, which is shed for you (Luke 22:20; cf. Hebrews 9:19,20).

In the ceremony that followed, God allowed Aaron, his sons and the elders to have a glimpse of His glory which must have been a tremendous faith building experience. Then, for the fifth time, Moses ascended Mount Sinai to spend a longer time with God. Now that the covenant had been sealed they needed something concrete to aid them in their worship, so this time on the Mount God instructed Moses about the Tabernacle and He Himself wrote down the ten commandments on the tablets of stone. Like Moses, we need to spend quality time with God so we may know His will, do as He instructs us and have our faith strengthened. He has given us His Holy Word and His Holy Spirit to aid us in worshipping Him.

Prayer for today: *Father God, we are spending time in Your Presence. Show us Your will and strengthen our faith.*

Read Exodus 25 *March 10*

Key Verse: Exodus 25:8 *"And let them make Me a sanctuary, that I may dwell among them."*

The Bible gives much detailed information about the tabernacle and everything involved in the Israelite form of worship. We read about it in the books of Exodus, all of Leviticus, part of Numbers and it is even explained in the New Testament in some chapters of Hebrews. Why is this so important that it takes up a large portion of the inspired Word?

(1) It had a divine origin and was instructed and commanded by God Himself (25:9). (2) In it we see the great, unlimited, sovereign God speaking in simple details with man on his comparatively very low level of understanding. God also came at man's own level in Jesus Christ. He reached out to mankind because of His love. (3) Many of the articles within symbolize the Lord Jesus who became flesh and dwelt among us (John 1:14). The New Testament infers that His dwelling was as a tabernacle in our midst (John 2:19; Hebrews 9:11). (4) All that was connected with the tabernacle is described in the New testament as a "copy and shadow of the heavenly things" (Hebrews 8:5; cf. 9:23; 10:1). (5) The relation is clearly seen when the veil in the Temple was torn at the time of Jesus' death on the cross (Matthew 27:51; Hebrews 10:19, 20; John 14:6). (6) We see with the light of the New Testament that through the tabernacle God revealed Himself to His people showing His holiness, glory, attributes and His relationship

with them, just as believers today find these through Jesus Christ.

With the Lord's abundant grace, He asked the Israelites to build His dwelling place from that which He had created. He could have done it Himself, but God always uses the humen vessel through whom He is to be glorified. He was pleased to have them build a place where they were encouraged to reverently go to repent of their sins, and become strengthened in their faith. With the New Covenant, we find that the Lord is present when just two or three are gathered in His name (Matt. 18:20). It is important for there to be a reverent gathering of fellow believers together: a place where one can be encouraged and built up in faith, a place where one can repent and make a public confession to follow God. The building of churches and other structures which glorify the Lord and lead people to Him is very important and needs the wholehearted support of the community of believers. God Himself encouraged the Israelites to give freewill offerings toward the building of the tabernacle; not giving because it was obligatory, but voluntarily out of a willing heart (25:2). We later learn that the Israelites gave generously much of which they received from the Egyptians at the time of their exodus (Ex. 12:35), and possibly the spoil taken from the defeated Amalekites. They not only gave, but all did their part and willingly pitched in to help in the construction (ch. 35).

The Lord first instructed Moses concerning the ark of the covenant which represented Jesus Christ. It was the most important piece of furniture in the Tabernacle, for it was where the atonement for their sins was made by the High Priest once a year (Leviticus 16). The mercy seat, upon which the blood was sprinkled, was on the top of the ark, between the cherubim which seem to be guards of the holiness of God. Jesus Christ is pictured in both the blood and the mercy seat which represents the means by which mankind comes to God, for from it the Lord Jesus intercedes for us.

On the table of showbread there was always to be a supply of twelve loaves which were to be consumed by the priests reverently before the Lord (Leviticus 24:5-9). This symbolized fellowship with God and reminded the Israelites of the necessity of continual communion with Him through the constantly renewed supply. We receive this communion with the Lord when we daily partake of His Holy Word and with prayer have fellowship with Jesus and spiritual renewal.

The seven-branched lampstand of pure hold was the only light within the tabernacle, just as Jesus is the light of the world (John 8:12). The lampstand symbolized the light or testimony that God's people were to have to the world. Today it is our responsibility as God's people to share His light with the world. In Israel, the almond tree is the first to come alive and blossom after the cold months, so the decorations of almond blossoms on the lampstand represent the new life through this Light. The lampstand's light source came from a lighted wick in the purest olive oil. The oil represents the Holy Spirit; when He is in us, He causes the light of Jesus to shine brightly through us drawing others unto Him.

Prayer for today: *Lord, Your Holy Spirit indwells us and we are Your tabernacle in this age. Light up our lives and shine brightly through us today.*

Read Exodus 26   *March 11*

Key Verse: Exodus 26:33 *"Then you shall bring the ark of the Testimony in there, behind the veil. The veil shall be a divider for you between the holy place and the Most Holy."*

There is much symbolic significance throughout the chapters which deal with the tabernacle. The Lord describes in detail exactly how everything should be done, thus showing the importance of the tabernacle and tent which covered it. God gave Moses the pattern for them while he was on Mount Sinai for the period of forty days, and instructed him to follow the pattern exactly as he had shown him. God may have revealed it to Moses through a vision, or, since we know God Himself inscribed the ten commandments, it is possible that He may have sketched the tabernacle and its articles for Moses, as well as verbally explaining them (26:30; Acts 7:44; Heb. 8:5). Everything was to be made with great beauty. The Lord who created the beautiful world for mankind was also interested that His people create a beautiful dwelling for Him among them.

The Lord desires that our lives, the temple in which dwells His Holy Spirit, have inner beauty and be pure as Christ was pure (1 Corinthians 6:19). In the same manner, the tabernacle and tent which covered it are symbolic of Jesus Christ. On the inside, the tabernacle was incredibly beautiful, but the exterior tent, although much larger, very well made, having more layers (including one middle layer dyed red which may symbolize blood and life), and of the best quality, was rough and common looking (Isaiah 53:26). The magnificence could not be seen from the outside, only upon entrance was the awesomeness to be experienced. Likewise, those who have not entered into the life of Christ do not see the full beauty of it.

The layers of the tent served to provide insulation and were to be provided in obedience to God, even though they may have not understood why it was to be done in this particular way, for example: why have an unseen layer of ram's skin dyed red? There may be times when we do not understand the reasoning behind God's instructions, however we must obey. Our finite minds cannot fathom the workings of the mind of God, but we can rest assured He has a good reason. The outermost layer of the tent, made of some sort of very fine leather, provided a water proof protection in times of bad weather.

God instructed that the curtains and veils be made of fine linen thread which was most probably cleansed to be pure white, for only the best and purest quality could be symbolic of the perfection of Christ. The blue, purple, and scarlet may represent Christ's heavenly origin, royalty, and the blood He shed to cover us and cleanse us from our sins. In the book of Revelation we find beautiful colours such as these used to describe the breathtaking heavenly glory. The cherubin signify the presence of God and His holiness.

The most lovely and elaborate veil was the one between the holy place and the Most Holy Place. It served as a divider to ensure privacy and was a symbol of exclusion. No man on his own merit could pass beyond it into the Most Holy presence of God. Only once a year, on the day of atonement, the high priest was permitted to enter and only if he was sprinkled with the blood of the sacrifice as propitiation for himself and all the people. With the crucifixion of Jesus Christ, the partition of the veil in the Temple at Jerusalem was ripped in two from top to bottom by the power God, signifying that the all-sufficient sacrifice had been made once and for all. Believers can now boldly approach the throne of God covered by the precious blood of Jesus, yet still there must be reverence for God's holiness.

Praise the Lord that the way has been opened into His presence!

Prayer for today: *Thank You, Lord, that through Your Cross the veil of separation was torn from top to bottom. Now we enter the Holy of Holies to pray. Hallelujah!*

Read Exodus 27   March 12

Key Verse: Exodus 27:20 *"And you shall command the children of Israel that they bring you pure oil of pressed olives for the light, to cause the lamp to burn continually."*

After the description of everything inside the tabernacle we read of the bronze altar situated in the large open area of the court that surrounded the tabernacle and tent. God intended all the people, not just the priests, to participate in devotion to Him, and this was the area where all were welcome. There the sinner could come to offer a sacrifice of appeasement with the blood of propitiation. Through this shed blood of the sacrifice the people of the covenant could come closer to their God, and in this fashion were able to truly worship and have communion with Him. The joy of their relationship and His blessings upon them came through this altar of repentance. It was made of the same wood as the ark and table of showbread, but whereas they were overlaid with gold, this altar was overlaid with bronze, a symbol of power and strength.

Christ, as the altar for His church, sanctified Himself (John 17:19) and through His shed blood and mediation, His people as well are sanctified (Hebrews 13:12). The blood of the sacrifice was applied to the horns of the altar (Leviticus 4:7), and they were used to tie the slaughtered animal sacrifice so that no pieces of the sanctified flesh would fall to the ground while burning. The grate all around the altar served as a further safeguard so that not a single portion of the sacrifice would be defiled. Even the ashes were collected, removed, and then treated with care. Those who are sanctified unto the Lord are not to become defiled with the sins and dirt of the world. The horns were also a symbol of refuge where one might flee for protection and there be judged (eg. Adonijah — 1 Kings 1:50-53).

The court area was enclosed by plain linen curtains that were about two and a half meters high, sufficient to provide privacy within. There was only one entrance into the tabernacle court area and only those Israelites who were ceremonially clean could enter, just as there is only one way to the Lord God today—through Jesus Christ who cleanses us. At this entrance-way there was a veil having the colours of blue, purple and scarlet embroidered in a similar, but less elaborate fashion as the other veils within the tabernacle. The court seems to picture the Church of Jesus Christ being separate from the rest of the world, yet still a part of the world. The enclosure was supported by pillars, representing the stability and strength of the church which is based upon a strong foundation. The curtains which made up the enclosure were made of clean fine linen which is said to be "the righteous acts of the saints" (Revelation 19:8).

The Psalmist longed to dwell and sing praises to the Lord in His courts and exclaimed that one day there was better than a thousand elsewhere (Psalm 84:). The physical enclosure, which could only hold a limited number of worshippers, has now been taken away by the atoning work of Jesus Christ. With the gospel, God has opened the way for everyone in every part of the world to come before Him in prayer through Jesus Christ. We may constantly dwell in the Lord's presence and continually offer unto Him the sacrifice of praise (Hebrews 13:15).

The continuously burning lamp in the tablernacle was to be a statute forever for the children of Israel, expressing the light of the Lord in His presence among them always. The most pure olive oil was used to fuel the light. Pure oil is seen in the Bible as a symbol of the Holy Spirit which should constantly burn within the believer, enabling those that worship the Lord to shine for Him.

Prayer for today: *Lord, thank You that we can enter into Your presence by the Holy Spirit to sing praise to You so that we will surely shine for You in this darkened world.*

Read Exodus 28 *March 13*

Key Verse: Exodus 28:12b *"So Aaron shall bear their names before the Lord on his two shoulders as a memorial."*

It was God's intention that all Israel be His priests (Ex. 19:6), but here we see that He appointed and set apart Aaron and his sons to this holy office so that there might be an orderly and effective form of worship. To show clearly that they were consecrated and sanctified for God's special service, He gave Moses detailed instructions concerning their beautiful and costly garments which would express the glory and beauty (radiance) of God (28:2). Those with God-given talents, whom He had also filled with the spirit of wisdom, were to make the artistic garments. The most beautiful was for the high priest. It is wonderful to see that many believers today wisely use thier talents to glorify the Lord.

The names of the twelve tribes upon the shoulder straps of the ephod and the breastplate represent all the children of Israel. This indicates that the high priest was their mediator who brought their names before the Lord. The names upon the shoulders signify that the priest bore the burdens of all Israel as he represented them before God. As well as being on this place of strength, they were also on his heart, so that he might plead their cause before God with compassion and wisdom. Although the Israelites were not permitted to enter the holy places, they were still brought there by their representatives, the high priest. The New Testament declares that Jesus is our High Priest, not according to the imperfect order of Aaron, but rather according to the order of Melchizedek (Heb. 7:11). With strength and compassion He upholds each individual believer before the Father so that we have the right to enter into the holiest, and by faith "sit together in the heavenly places in Christ Jesus" (Ephesians 2:6). What an honour God has bestowed on the believers, His spiritual priests.

The individual names inscribed upon the various precious stones signified that each person is unique and important to God. When the Light (Jesus), shines upon these gems (the children of God), they shine for all to see. Even though the stones represent weak and imperfect people, they become radiant and acceptable because of the Mediator that bears them before God. What a comforting thought to know we are seen by God through the light of Jesus who always shines brightly before Him to represent us.

The robe of the ephod was entirely blue representing heavenly glory. On the bottom of this robe were alternating pomegranates and bells. They may represent fruitbearing and testimony. The believers, God's "royal priesthood" (1 Peter 2:9), are to walk before God with the evidence of bearing fruit, bringing others into the Kingdom of God and walking boldly with an open and resounding testimony for Him. The plate of pure gold upon the priest's forehead clearly stated that he was consecrated to God and served as a constant reminder of his acceptance and responsibility before Him. It should remind believers that in their life of service to God they too are meant to be "holiness to the Lord". We do not wear a sign such as this, yet our whole life should be holy and attest to our consecration to God, along with wearing the garments of salvation, righteousness (Isaiah 61:10) and praise.

The Lord must be shown the greatest respect and reverence; one way the priests were to show this was in their modesty; while serving Him the priests were to wear linen undergarments (28:42; cf. 20:26). The priests were warned to obey God and always be properly attired when ministering in the tabernacle; if they were disobedient the penalty was death (28:43). The complete and perfect priestly attire glorified God, thus representing Jesus Christ's perfection, radiance, and glory.

The "Urim and Thummim" (Hebrew — 'lights and perfections'), placed in the centre of the breastplate are a mystery. However, we do know they were given by God to be used as a means of revealing His will. They were consulted when a major decision or judgment was to be made (cf. Ezra 2:63; Num. 27:21; Deut. 33:8-10; 1 Sam. 28:6). This indicates the priests' importance: they brought God's answers and divine solutions to the people. Jesus is our Light to whom we may go to when faced with decisions. We can have faith that He will illuminate us concerning the will of God.

Prayer for today: *Dear Heavenly Father, thank You that the symbolism of the Old has become the reality of the New. We bear upon shoulders of intercession the names of our loved ones before You. May Your holiness adorn the inner person.*

Exodus 29 *March 14*

Key Verse: Exodus 29:42 *"This shall be a continual burnt offering... at the door of the tabernacle...where I will meet you to speak with you."*

Before Aaron and his sons could be involved in active service to God, they were to be consecrated to Him. This was done through an elaborate ceremony of sanctification in which Moses officiated as the mediator. They were (1) to be washed with water signifying **purity**. In the Bible washing has spiritual symbolism: cleansing by the Word (Ephesians 5:26); the "washing of regeneration" (Titus 3:5). Jesus "washed us from our sins by His own blood" (Rev. 1:5); and because He is our High Priest, we can draw near to God "in full assurance of faith, having our hearts sprinkled from an evil conscience and our bodies washed with pure water" (Heb. 10:22). (2) The priests were to be **set apart** by being arrayed in their holy garments, and (3) anointed with oil, signifying their **sanctification** and **empowerment** for effective ministry by God the Spirit. In the Bible oil represents the Holy Spirit. Aaron the high priest, as a type of Christ, was anointed before the sacrifice by oil being poured upon his head (29:7), just as Christ was anointed by the Spirit descending upon Him (Luke 3:22; 4:1) before He shed His own blood in sacrifice. Aaron's sons were anointed after the sacrifice was made (29:20, 21). Likewise, after Christ's perfect sacrifice His servants were filled with the Holy Spirit as an anointing to His service (Acts 2:1-4). (4) The sacrifices and the use of the blood were the most important part of the ceremony. These not only made atonement for Aaron and his sons, but were for the purification of the altar as well. The blood applied to the various right parts of their bodies were signs of consecration to God by the power of redemption and the work of the Holy Spirit. The blood was applied to the ear, for they were to listen to God; upon the hand to serve Him; and upon the foot to walk in His ways and in holiness. At every sacrifice, Aaron and his sons were to put their hands upon the animal's head which is a clear indication that their sins and guilt were to be laid upon the sacrificial animal with which they identified themselves. Jesus offered Himself unto death as the all-sufficient, final, and perfect sacrifice. He lovingly and willingly became our substitute to bear our guilt and sins, taking the punishment we deserve. (5) The wave offering signified the offering of their lives to God in **complete consecration**. Since God is holy, all those people or things dealing with Him are to be holy as well. (6) The last part of the ceremony involved eating the sacrificial meal, representing **fellowship** with God. Once atonement was made for their sins, having been made holy before God, they could enter into true communion with Him (29:33).

This impressive ceremony of sanctifying the priests and the altar was repeated for seven days. It made the whole nation realize the holiness of God and the importance of high calling of the priests and their duties.

The establishment of the tabernacle, the priesthood, and the daily sacrifices was to assure God's continual presence in dwelling among them. The continual burnt offerings of the lambs, one every morning and a second in the evening, meant they were daily meeting with God (29:42) and therefore He would be among them to speak with them (29:44, 45). These sacrifices came up to the Lord as a sweet aroma (29:41), something which appeased Him and through which the people gained His acceptance. They typify the continual intercession of Jesus Christ before the Father. With these offerings God said, "I will meet you (plural form) to speak with you (singular form)".

When we pray and worship God it gives Him the opportunity to speak with us as individuals and touch our hearts in a personal way. These daily offerings teach us that each day, ideally every morning and night (yet not to be forgotten during the course of the day as well), we should offer up to God the spiritual sacrifice of prayer and praise. For those who follow the Lord, times of fellowship with God, when fed by His Word, should be considered the most necessary and important activity of the day. In so doing, the Lord dwells among His children.

Jesus has promised his workers: "I am with you always" (Matt. 28:20). Hallelujah!

Prayer for today: *Lord, as our Eternal High Priest, You have presented Your own Blood before the Mercy Seat. Help us today to fulfill Your purpose in our fellowship with You.*

Key Verse: Exodus 30:7 *"Aaron shall burn on it sweet incense every morning (and 'at twilight,' verse 8) when he tends the lamps...".*

The altar of incense was very important. It was covered with pure gold and situated in the Holy Place directly in front of the ark but before the veil. It is called an altar, although no blood sacrifices are offered upon it. God considers prayer and praise a sacrifice (Psalm 141:2; 107:22; Heb. 13:15); something necessary in our relationship with Him. At the same time the priest tended the lamps, he was to tend the incense. The lamp represents the word of God, and the incense represents prayer. From this we learn that prayer, praise and reading God's word should go together. God desires the constant praise and worship of His creation. In tending the incense, the priest faced the mercy seat and directed the aroma toward it, although it could not be seen because of the veil. In like manner, we cannot physically see the throne of God, yet with faith we direct our prayers to the Lord. In the Bible, the prayers of the saints are compared to "golden bowls full of incense" (Rev. 5:8) which are then, through our mediator, the Lord Jesus, offered up to the throne of God (Rev. 8:3), that they may be acceptable. In this manner, God hears and answers our prayers according to His will.

The sweet aroma would constantly flow into the Holy of Holies and encompass the mercy seat. Likewise, Christ our advocate, always appears in the presence of God for us. The offering of Himself on the cross was "for a sweet-smelling aroma" (Ephesians 5:2) which continues to appease God's wrath against us which we as sinners deserve, but instead, commends us for righteousness. Jesus Christ (symbolized by the incense) through the believer (the gold censer which housed the incense) "diffuses the fragrance of His knowledge in every place. For we are to God the fragrance of Christ" (2 Cor. 2:14-16). The perfect proportions and ingredients combined to make the incense was a divine invention. It was not to be copied, for there could be no counterfeit; just as there is only one divinely given Christ, who is "most holy to the Lord" (30:10).

There is a link between the altar of incense and the bronze altar. The fire for burning the incense was taken from the bronze altar. The same fire, which God initially gave, burnt the offering and also brought a sweet aroma to Him. This holy fire was to be guarded so it would not die out. Once a year the blood from the bronze altar was to be applied to the horns of the incense altar as a rite of purification, for it came in contact with sinful people and, so required cleansing and renewed sanctification by the blood. We must keep ourselves pure, cleansed by the blood of Jesus, and never let the fire of the Lord be extinguished from our lives so that we are able to pray and worship Him in the right way. Before the high priest would make atonement in the Holy of Holies once a year, by sprinkling the mercy seat with the blood from the sacrifice, he was first to enter with the incense that the ark might be enveloped in its cloudy smoke (Lev. 16:13, 14). This may represent Christ's intervention and intercession which precedes our forgiveness by God and acceptance to Him.

The ransom money, the price of a life, (30:11-16) was the same for all the Israelites, regardless of their economic position. In other offerings, they gave according to their means, but this was not a free-will offering; it was obligatory, for all benefited from the tabernacle and its services, especially the grace God granted on the day of atonement. Since all were sinners and have the same need for Christ, this ransom for their soul had to be the same. Several Jewish expositors believe this was a yearly tribute to be paid to the tabernacle (and later to the temple in Jerusalem) which Moses began, upon the instruction of God, when the first census was taken.

In the New Testament Jesus was required to make this payment called the "temple tax". Although He had good reason to be excluded, He paid it so none would be offended (Matt. 17:24-27). As well as providing for the on-going expenses of the tabernacle and the priesthood, the ransom money reminded them that their life came from God. Refusal to pay it could result in God's wrath and judgment through plagues (30:12).

The laver, or washing basin, held a large quantity of water to be used only by the priests. Those involved in service to God must be pure. It was not only a part of the priest's consecration ceremony, but was a daily cleansing. Each new day we need to purify our hearts to draw nearer to God (James 4:8). This practice was to help them understand the reverence for God and His holiness.

The holy oil and incense were to be made by skilled people and intended for sacred use only, not for any common purposes. The sacred things of God are not to be mocked or taken lightly, nor is any counterfeit to be made. Once again, a reverence for God's holiness and ordinances is stressed.

Prayer for today: O God, we offer up the sacrifice of prayer and praise. May we daily direct this aroma toward Your Throne. We reverence Your Holiness and we carefully approach Your Throne having been washed through the reading of your Holy Word.

Read Exodus 31   March 16

Key Verse: *"I have appointed...and...put wisdom in the hearts of all who are gifted artisans, that they may make all that I have commanded you."* (31:6)

God did not leave Moses alone with just the plans for the tabernacle; He was interested to see the plans carried out in the exact way He had prescribed. Therefore, along with providing the materials, He also provided the people with the necessary skills, for those whom God calls for a purpose He also equips to do the job. He called the gifted craftsman, Bezaleel, to be chief over the construction of the tabernacle and its furnishings. Bezaleel was the first man in the Bible ever spoken of as being "filled...with the Spirit of God" (31:3). He needed this divine empowerment, wisdom, understanding, and knowledge for the important work he was to do for the Lord. God also gave him an able, Spirit-filled assistant, Aholiab. They were willing and honoured to be used of God in this manner, were as many other "gifted artisans" who came under their supervision. All the workers were divinely motivated. Through the Spirit, their natural, yet God-given abilities, were enhanced to carefully, with unity and sensitivity, carry out His plans diligently and precisely as He had commanded.

When God calls believers today, the most important thing is that they be **willing** to perform the task and bring Him glory, having confidence that He will equip them by His Spirit. While enslaved in Egypt, one of the most advanced nations of their day, many of the Israelites would have learned the necessary skills for doing the delicate and ingenious work required. Little did they know that what they had learned during their slavery would one day be used by God for a greater service: to build what was to become the centre of society for their own nation. Jesus Christ commanded those who followed Him to build His Church, the tabernacle of the Lord today, but before they were able, they were first filled with His Spirit. Since this new tabernacle is greater (Heb.9:11), so also are the divinely given spiritual gifts which are distributed as God wills to each member of the body of Christ (1 Cor. 12:1, 27) for the purpose of building up His Church.

After God finished telling Moses all His plans concerning the tabernacle, thus giving the go-ahead, "according to all that I have commanded you they shall do" (31:11), He immediately reemphasized the fourth commandment, "surely [nevertheless] My Sabbaths you shall keep" (31:13). The people were not to be in such a great rush, nor so zealous to build the Lord's tabernacle that they would disregard their day of rest. This important command was to be a sign which distinguished God's people from all others. Its observance proved their obedience to God and respect for Him. Its observance was foundational for the whole law. The reason for the sabbath was God's example in creation (31:17). It was instituted before any other laws (Gen. 2:2,3) and it was given as central in the moral law (Ex. 20:8-11). It was restated in the judicial law (Ex:23:10-12), and here we find it included in the ceremonial law. It was given for mankind's benefit (see Mark 2:27) as well as for the honour and service of God. It was to be sanctified, a holy day, not a common day, just as the holy incense and oil were not for a common use. The seriousness of breaking these commands was expressed in the severity of the penalty, that of death, being "cut off" from among the living (30:33, 38; 31:14).

Thank God that today we live under the dispensation of grace (Eph. 3:2) with the intercession of Christ and His forgiveness. This and most other outward observances of the Law have been translated in the New Testament to inward spiritual evidences of discipleship (Rom. 2:28, 29; Col. 2:16,17; Heb. 8:10).

Before Moses descended the mountain, after communing with the Lord for forty days, God gave him the two promised tablets of stone (Ex. 24:12), upon which He wrote with His finger (an act of the Holy Spirit) the ten commandments, thus indicating their extreme holiness. Moses was to take them down for all to see and then place them in the ark as a reminder of their covenant with God. Now, concerning believers, the new house of Israel, God has said, "I will put My laws in their mind and write them on their hearts; and I will be their God, and they shall be My people" (Heb.8:10).

Prayer for today: *We want to present back to You, O God, the gifts which You have bestowed upon us for the building of Your kingdom.*

Read Exodus 32 March 17

Key Verse: Exodus 32:32 *"Yet now, if You will forgive their sin — but if not, I pray, blot me out of Your book which You have written."*

It had been thirty-nine or forty days since Moses had left the people below and ascended Mount Sinai. They probably thought he was dead, for they may have lacked faith that God was able to care for Moses and provide him with food and water. When Moses, their mediator was absent they might have believed that God was absent too, however God saw all their actions (32:7) and He even saw their hearts. For this reason, they pressured Aaron to make them a god to go before them on their journey. He was probably afraid to stand up against them. He admitted they were "set on evil" (32:22), so there was no telling what they might do if he refused them. Still he had no backbone to stay firm and uphold the Lord's commands. Aaron did not have the communion with God which Moses had, and he had to be strong, withstand temptation, and lead in that difficult nation.

The calf, or a young bull, was one of the main gods in Egypt; it was called Apis, which represented fertility and strength. The Israelites held a feast in its honour, accompanied by lewd dancing and immorality connected with the pagan fertility cult. How could this awful apostasy of breaking the first two important commandments come so soon after their miraculous deliverance, the thundering of God's voice, and after they had all agreed to obey Him and enter into a covenant relationship with Him? As God told Moses, they were truly a "stiff-necked people" (32:9), the expression coming from a stubborn ox or horse that refuses to be turned by the reins.

Because their wickedness in breaking the covenant provoked the wrath of God, He told Moses of His intention to wipe out all Israel and start fresh with just Moses and his descendants as His chosen people (32:10). This was a real test of Moses' character and his love for his people. He responded in the right way. Preferring Israel's preservation over his own honour, he interceded on their behalf, recalling God's promise to the patriarchs, but Moses' main concern was for the honour of God (32;12, 25). Because of his desperate plea, the Lord agreed to not totally destroy the Israelites, but immediate discipline and punishment was still required for the unrepentant. The wickedness of our society provokes the wrath of God who would consume the sinners were it not for the prayers of the saints and the mediation of His Son. God is truly merciful; He does not take pleasure in seeing men die, but rather takes pleasure in forgiving those sinners who come unto Him. Surely Aaron repented, or else God would not have allowed him to become the high priest, but here we see him trying to make excuses and blame the people (32:22-24). Yet, Moses considered him responsible as he had been in charge during Moses' absence.

The actual sight of the people's sin affected Moses more than hearing of it. With righteous indignation, he threw down and broke the stone tablets, representing the covenant which had already been broken by their hearts and deeds. He made the people internalize their sin by drinking water into which he had thrown the powder from the golden calf which he had burned. Still most remained unrepentant and stubborn, for only the tribe of Levi quickly expressed shame and repentance in going over to the side of the Lord with Moses (32:26). Punishment followed those who did not respond to the call of grace and mercy; three thousand men died by the sword.

Today, God is mercifully waiting for people's repentance and acceptance of His new covenant with His Son Jesus before the great and terrible judgment day. Let us be like Moses (not Aaron, who went along with the crowd) and lead others to walk in the way of righteousness. If we do not, we can be held responsible for their punishment (Ezekiel 33:8). Moses, as their mediator, tried to make atonement by offering himself to die for the people if it would cause God to forgive and restore them (32:32). This, however, was not God's plan. Only Jesus Christ could make the all-sufficient atonement for the sins of others. God told Moses that the sinner alone would be punished, not he, and God accomplished this by sending a plague among them. Moses' intercession, however, preserved the nation of Israel and their entrance into Canaan under God's protection. Our fervent prayers do make a difference, so be encouraged and keep on praying!

Prayer for today: *Almighty God, help me to learn to intercede in prayer for others. Thank You for our mighty intercessor, the Lord Jesus Christ.*

Read Exodus 33   March 18

Key Verse: Exodus 33:14 *And He said, "My Presence will go with you, and I will give you rest."*

What a beautiful chapter of the grace of God! Upon the fervent intercession of Moses, the Lord consented to let the Israelites live, instead of destroying them as they deserved (33:5), and He permitted them to continue their journey to the Promised Land. The difference this time in their traveling was that His own presence would not be among them, only a created angel would go with them, not the same Messenger as before in whom was God's name (Ex. 23:20-22), the second person of the trinity, Jesus Christ. Even permission to enter the Promised Land did not bring joy if God did not go with them. Certainly true joy only comes if God is present in our midst. The Israelites were grieved by this judgment upon them for their apostasy.

Finally, they began to realize the gravity of their sin, its consequences, and the weight of God's judgment. Moses felt that if the very presence of God would not go with them, then it was best not to go on at all (33:15). The people must have felt the same way, for they mourned at the thought of it (33:3,4). In His mercy, the Lord called them to repentance by asking them to remove their jewelry (the sign of a penitent and mourner). The golden calf had been made from their jewelry, now they were asked to remove them in token of their shame and remorse. After they obeyed, God would decide the extent of mercy He would grant them (33:5).

The tent which Moses pitched outside the camp was the one from which he would counsel the people and where He would commune with God. It was a temporary sanctuary until the permanent tabernacle was built about seven months later (Ex. 40:2,17). It seemed the removal of this tent from among the people meant they were no longer worthy of it. It also served to symbolize God's judgment of separation from Him, because of their sin. However, anyone who sought the Lord with a pure heart was welcome to go there. God is not too far that it is impossible to reach Him, for He has always provided a way for those who sincerely seek Him. Those whose hearts go up to meet God, can be sure that He will graciously come down to meet with them, just as the pillar of cloud, signifying His presence, descended to meet with Moses (33:9). This separation seemed to have stirred a longing in the hearts of the Israelites to restore the closeness with God they once had. When Moses went to this tent the people watched him and stood in respect. They must have had a hope of restoration, for when they saw the cloudy pillar they worshipped God while standing outside their tents. This act served as an important public confession of faith in God.

Moses was so close to God that they communed "face to face" like friends (33:11). This expression may mean a form, or similitude of the Lord, but it was not the actual sight of the full glory of God which Moses later desired to see (33:18). Before he was bold enough to ask such a favour of God, he was first encouraged upon hearing that he found grace in His sight (33:12), and, with his persistent intercession, the Lord's agreement to once again make Israel His people by accompanying them with His presence (33:14). The text seems to indicate that previously the Lord had disowned them because they had broken the covenant (32:7; 33:140. Moses' continued intercession resembles that which Jesus Christ does for us before God; He procures the removal of the curse, thus saving us from destruction, and obtains for us an assured life of blessing and everlasting happiness in the presence of God from which comes true peace and rest.

Such grace and mercy should encourage us in our faith and cause us to desire an even closer relationship with God, as Moses did in his request to see His full glory. This request was not totally possible, as God in His understanding and mercy explained: no mere mortal could see His full brilliance and survive (33:20). This privilege is reserved for the believer's future life in eternity (1 John 3:2). God answered Moses that His sovereign goodness and mercy alone, which He brings upon those whom He chooses (cf. Romans 9:15,16,18), should be sufficient to see His glory (33:19). God did permit Moses to catch a glimpse of the afterglow of His splendor as He passed by, but His full glory was so great that He had to place Moses in the cleft of the rock and shield him. That was the Rock of Horeb, which is said to represent Jesus (1 Corinthians 10:4). In the cleft of this Rock, God protects those who are hid in Jesus and from this Rock, Jesus Christ, we have the sight and knowledge of the glory of God (cf.John 1:18).

Prayer for today: Lord, we throw ourselves on Your mercy. Please let us see Your glory. We have heartfelt thanks for Your gift of Your Son. In Him we have beheld Your glory.

Read Exodus 34   March 19

Key Verse: Exodus 34:6 *"The Lord, the Lord God, merciful and gracious, longsuffering, and abounding in goodness and truth...".*

Before going up alone to meet with God early the next morning, Moses was told to make himself ready (34:2) and to cut new stone tablets to replace the ones he had broken. God, in His grace, would once again inscribe His moral law upon them. This was the first act of God in His reconciliation with Israel. Likewise, when we are reconciled to God He writes His laws upon our hearts (Heb. 8:10). But first, like Moses who was required to prepare the tablets, we must prepare our hearts that they be open and tender to receive the law of God. The rough stone tablets became a beautiful expression of God's love and acceptance for the Israelites. In the same manner, when God writes upon our hearts we should show forth His beauty and love within us.

Once Moses ascended the mountain, God immediately came down to meet him in a pillar of cloud, thus veiling the brilliance of His glory. Here God made Himself known to Moses in the fuller way he desired (33:18). As God passed by Moses, He expressed the glory of His mercy, grace, patience, goodness, and forgiveness which all stem from the great love He has for His people. To know God we do not have to visually see Him; we know Him by His character, attributes, and experiencing His presence all in faith believing. His "mercy for thousands" implies the universal extent of His grace. Although the

Israelites were His special people at that time, He still was good and merciful to others. At the same time, the Lord is just and holy, and will not clear the guilty — those who do not repent (34:7). This part of verse seven can also be translated: "forgiving iniquity, transgression, and sin which by no means goes unnoticed".

The Lord is all-seeing and all-knowing. No one should think they can hide their wrongdoings from Him. Those who do not repent, and thereby do not reverse the curse upon them, cause sinfulness (because of the bad influence,) among their descendants as well, even until the third or fourth generation. This is true until the Spirit of the Lord draws one unto repentance and thus the future course of their family may be changed from a curse to a blessing. Moses wanted reconfirmation from God that the Israelites, His inheritance, would see His blessings and His forgiveness. God's newly revealed glory caused Moses to bow low and worship Him (34:8), and he prayed that God would indeed pardon their iniquity and go with them (34:9). Since they were a "stiff-necked people", they especially needed His presence among them to keep them on the straight and narrow. Although the Lord had already promised these things, Moses was seeking the ratification of them and the Lord did this by renewing the covenant with the Israelites (34:10). This was done through Moses as their mediator, likewise the New Covenant of grace with believers is made through Jesus Christ. There are two main points in the covenant that God stressed since on these very things they had already failed: (1) "you shall worship no other god" (34:14) and (2) "you shall make no molded gods" (34:17). They were not to make any treaties with the heathen nations, nor allow any intermarriage which is a compromise leading to spiritual downfall.

During this second forty days and nights, the Lord reiterated several rules He had given concerning the observance of the sabbath and other feasts (34:18-26; see comments on Ex. 23:10-19), plus some additional information. This time Moses gained more knowledge of God and saw more of His glory. In the closing period upon the mountain, the Lord once again commanded Moses to write the book of the Law. This was so the people would have something concrete that they might learn and know what God expected of them, and to have the written word to pass on to their future generations. Would the people remain faithful this time while Moses was absent, and trust that God could provide all his needs? It is impossible for a person to go without food and water for forty days, but God supernaturally sustained Moses. This time the Israelites passed the test. Moses descended the mountain with good news of reconciliation to those anxiously awaiting the Lord's reply and he was honoured by God to carry down His written Word to them. What an honour it is to give the words of God to others! Moses' face was shining with the glory of the Lord, a sign that he had met with God and his mediation on their behalf had been accepted. The people must have been filled with great joy, but at the same time they experienced a much needed fear and reverence for God and His holiness.

Prayer for today: *Thank You Father for Your forgiveness. Please keep us faithful to You. Your goodness leads us to repentance.*

Read Exodus 35 & 36 *March 20*

Key Verse: Exodus 35:21 *"Then everyone came whose heart was stirred, and everyone whose spirit was willing, and they brought the Lord's offering for the work of the tabernacle of meeting, for all its service, and for the holy garments."*

Here begins the account of the actual building of the tabernacle. Before Moses gave any details about it, he first reminded the Israelites of the importance and obligation of sabbath observance (35:2,3). Even in their enthusiasm to build the house of God, they were not to disregard this law of rest and waiting upon God one day out of seven. There is a spiritual and physical danger of not taking a day of rest because of being over-zealous, and over-industrious. The body and soul absolutely require this rest. God, who made us and knows us, has provided for this need by His sabbath day.

Moses was faithful to the Lord and to the people by telling them exactly the Lord's commands. He had been previously prevented from doing this by the incident of the golden calf. Now the people's hearts were ready to receive the Law and the careful instructions about the tabernacle. Moses did not pressure anyone to give to the building fund, he merely laid before them the need and they of their own accord and good will responded (35:21). He stressed that the gifts were to come from a willing heart (35:5). The Lord is pleased to see a cheerful giver (2 Cor. 9:7) and pleased to accept offerings which support His work.

Moses must have been thrilled to see the terrific response of all the people. Every person could contribute in one way or another as an individual expression of faith and worship. Along with willingly giving their time and talents to help, they also gave much more material than was required, until Moses even had to tell them to stop. It seems they gave out of a sacrificial spirit. If Moses or the others in leadership over the building project had been greedy and desiring to enrich themselves, they would have allowed the people to continue giving even after the need was met. But they were honest and faithful to the glory of God. Believers today should imitate the attitude of Moses and the Israelites in their giving; in such a way the Lord's work would be mightily advanced.

Now that Bezaleel and Aholiab had all the materials needed, they were able to start the construction. If they alone were to have done this great task, it would have taken years, but God provided them with much help and filled these helpers as well as themselves with the spirit of wisdom, that even their natural capabilities would be improved. God's Spirit enabled Bezaleel and Aholiab with the gift of teaching and also enabled the others to learn from them so that the work would be done exactly as God instructed. Many people in various capacities and with various gifts were needed to see God's desire accomplished, just like it is among the believers in Christ today: all have a different function, but all are necessary. To see the work accomplished it is important that our God-given abilities be put into action.

Much of the instruction that Moses gave the people is repeated here exactly as it had been given first to Moses by God (Ex. 25-31). This was not useless repetition, but an emphasis that they might carefully adhere to God's word. Without obedience, no amount of labour on the tabernacle or sacrifices offered could be acceptable to God.

The best free-will offering one can give to the Lord today is ones' life, offered to the service of God to be used where needed. All the Israelites happily brought gifts to the Lord. In the same way we who believe and love the Lord should desire to bring Him those precious gifts of souls into His kingdom to make up the gospel tabernacle of Christ; we can never give too much. In the house of the Lord there is room for all. In 1 Peter chapter 2 verses 4 and 5 we read: "Coming to Him (the Lord Jesus) as to a living stone, rejected indeed by men, but chosen by God and precious, you also, as living stones, are being built up a spiritual house, a holy priesthood, to offer up spiritual sacrifices acceptable to God through Jesus Christ."

Prayer for today: *O Lord, we offer our lives unto You for Your purpose. Help us to show this in practical terms in faithful service and offerings for Your cause and kingdom.*

Read Exodus 37 & 38   March 21

Key Verse: Exodus 38:22 *"Bezaleel...of the tribe of Judah, made all that the Lord had commanded Moses"*

Throughout these chapters, we are told that all the furnishings were made by Bezaleel. As the foreman, he was responsible for seeing that all the work was done in exact accordance to God's instructions. We know he had tremendous help and that he taught others the necessary skills, so "he" as the head man had all these articles made, along with doing a great deal of work himself, especially the honor of making the important articles in the holy places. The building began with the most important furnishings; firstly, those found in the Most Holy Place (the ark, mercy seat, and above it, the cherubim; see comments on Exodus 25:10-22), and then those items found in the holy place (the table of showbread, lampstand, and the altar of incense; Exodus 25:23-39; 30:1-10). Also at this point the holy anointing oil was prepared (Exodus 30:23-33); then the outer court (Exodus 27:9-19) with the bronze altar and laver (Exodus 27:1-8; 30:18-21) were constructed.

We learn that the bronze laver was made from the polished bronze mirrors that the "serving women" donated (38:8). These women must have played an important role, for they were worthy of mention. They were devoted to the work of the tabernacle and assembled at the entrance. They were probably doing the important task of caring for the needs of the workers, such as preparing and offering food and drink. This, their "labour of love" (Hebrews 6:10) and their gifts of bronze mirrors (a valuable treasured possession for women in those days) did not go unnoticed by God or Moses. Those mirrors, which once reflected natural faces, were transformed into a holy item which reminded those who served God of their need for spiritual cleansing in order to reflect His glory.

It must have been quite a task to take inventory and audit all the materials that went into making the tabernacle. Aaron's son Ithamar was entrusted with this responsibility (38:21). He was probably chosen to do this because he was well-organized, and a very intelligent accountant. The cost of the building and all its furnishings cannot be accurately interpreted in today's economy, but certainly it totalled an enormous sum. It was a magnificent monument expressing the dedication and respect of the Israelites to their God. It is significant that the only obligatory offering used in its construction was the ransom money (38:26; cf. Exodus 30:11-16). This seems to indicate that the faithful and obedient redeemed are the foundation of the tabernacle.

We must not think that the repetitive passages found here are of no purpose, for Moses as other writers of Scripture, wrote under the inspiration of the Holy Spirit and everything in the Bible has a purpose. Moses wrote with the Israelites in mind. It was necessary for them to hear and read over and over again these hidden and holy treasures which they were not permitted to view. To visualize them in their minds they needed detailed descriptions. In writing them again, Moses showed the great care taken to make the articles exactly as God had ordered. The people could compare the original instructions with the written record of the work actually done, and thereby observe how exactly they agreed. In doing this, Moses proved to be faithful unto the Lord, even in the small details of all His commands (cf. Hebrews 3:5). We learn from Him, to highly respect and obey all God's commands. Not only was Moses found faithful, but so were the workers who served to be a good example, even to believers today.

Prayer for today: *Almighty God, grant that we may take great care in all that we do for You. Thank You for being interested in the details of our lives and our service.*

Read Exodus 39   March 22

Key Verse: Exodus 39:43 *"Then Moses looked over all the work, and indeed they had done it; as the Lord had commanded...And Moses blessed them."*

Finally the holy priestly garments were carefully made, giving full care to details in their preparation. In reading about the way they were made, we find that it corresponds to the original instructions given by God to Moses (Ex.28). Here, more than in any other passage concerning the articles involved in the tabernacle, we are told that upon the completion of each item they were found to be done just "as the Lord had commanded Moses" (39:5,7,21,26,29,31). They are called "garments of ministry" or "of service" (39:1), since all who serve God, especially those who have a ministerial capacity, must take extreme care to be obedient in the observance of the Lord's commands.

Those who are honoured to wear the holy garments of service are expected to serve others, just as did our great High Priest, Jesus Christ who came as a servant to the world (Matthew 20:28). Believers in Him are said in the Bible to be spiritual priests whose garments are righteousness (Rev. 19:8; further symbolic significance is explained in the comments on Exodus 28). "Holiness to the Lord" is the motto and banner of believers. It was written upon the high priest's crown for all to see, just as it should be clearly evident in the conduct and conversation of believers today. They are the spiritual priesthood of Jesus Christ and as such must bear the image of God's holiness and thereby be Christ-like.

The completion of all the work took a relatively short period of time (possibly between five to seven months) considering the greatness of the project. All the people were enthusiastic, zealous, unified, and pleased to be of service to their God, therefore the work was finished quickly, though done very carefully. Later on, Hezekiah would restore the temple, and upon its completion we are told that he and all the people "rejoiced that God prepared the people, since the events took place so suddenly" (2 Chronicles 29:36). In the same way, at this time, God prepared the people. The work was amazingly finished, and there must have been even greater rejoicing, for this was the first time the house of the Lord had been established among them. The Spirit of God was the actual designer, architect, builder and teacher. He worked through Bezaleel, Aholiab, and even all the workers involved; they were divinely guided and thus prevented from making grave mistakes which would have held up the construction. Since they followed God's orders exactly, it must have been a breathtaking sight to behold, for it was actually conceived in the mind of God, and could never hope to improve upon it or beautify it. In the work of the Lord everything must be done according to His will, and then the outcome will be beautiful.

Out of respect for Moses, the people brought all the finished work to him that he might compare it with the instructions he had received from God. Every piece was mentioned again (39:33-41) for they were all very important in God's service. Likewise, God is interested in and knows by name each person dedicated to Him and His service. Each individual's offerings and works are important and do not go unnoticed by Him, no matter how small or insignificant they may seem to others.

The climax came when Moses viewed all the work and found it done exactly "as the Lord commanded" (39:43; the key verse). For him, all the people, and especially for the Lord, this was to their great pleasure and satisfaction. The finished product must have thrilled Moses tremendously, and after seeing it, he gave a blessing (more valuable than wages) to those who laboured. As well as receiving a blessing, those workers were honoured to be a part of God's work and would receive much benefit from the tabernacle and its services. We as God's children should ensure everything we do is in His will and done in His way, that we might bring Him glory, attain His pleasure and satisfaction, and with that receive His blessing.

Prayer for today: *O God, our Lord and Saviour Jesus Christ said He would build His Church. Build in my life according to Your blueprints so that You will some day say, to the glory of Jesus Christ, "Well done".*

Read Exodus 40   *March 23*

Key Verse: Exodus 40:34 *"Then the cloud covered the tabernacle of meeting, and the glory of the Lord filled the tabernacle."*

Now that all the required material for the tabernacle and tent and every piece of furniture was ready and made according to the Lord's instructions, it only required assembling. But before that could happen Moses was waiting to hear from God, so that everything would be done in His way and in His prescribed timing. Sometimes servants of the Lord tend to be anxious to see things happening in His work, and rush excitedly into action without first hearing from God and getting the "go ahead". Before any important step be taken, we need to follow Moses' example and wait on God. If we do not, the Lord's blessing may be withheld.

In these chapters we have learned that the way of blessing is that of obedience and faithfulness. Moses did not have to wait long before the Lord gave him the appointed day as "the first day of the first month" (40:2), just two weeks before the Passover and almost one year after the Israelites had left Egypt (cf. Numbers 9:1-5). Then the Lord told Moses exactly how the tabernacle was to be set up; once everything was in their proper place, they could be anointed with oil and thus sanctified for God's service. To be sanctified and anointed by the Lord, we must first be found where the Lord wants us to be — in His will. Finally Moses was told the manner in which to consecrate the priests (40:3-15). Again it is stressed that Moses was obedient and "according to all that the Lord had commanded him, so he did" (40:16).

We read that all the work of setting up the tabernacle is attributed to Moses, since he was the chief overseer. The Levites were responsible to set up the tabernacle (cf. Numbers 3:21-39), so here, for the first time, Moses was showing them how it was to be done and with much man-power it was probably accomplished in less than a day. Moses also, although not a priest like Aaron and his sons, showed them the proper way to serve the Lord in the tabernacle, since he was especially appointed and ordained by God to do so. Once they learned from him, he entrusted all the duties to them so he could attend to his own divine appointment of judging and leading the people of the Lord.

The newly erected tabernacle and tent was but an empty, useless shell until the Lord's glory, veiled by the pillar of cloud, descended upon it, and came to dwell within. This awesome manifestation was a visible sign of God's acceptance of their work and a clear indication of His presence among them. Rays of light from God's glorious presence must have beamed forth from the cloud, for even Moses could not enter at that time (40:35). Our Lord Jesus, however, whom God caused to draw near, has "not entered the holy places made with hands, which are copies of the true, but into heaven itself, now to appear in the presence of God for us" (Hebrews 9:24).

Just as God promised the Israelites (Exodus 33:14), He now came fulfilling His desire and theirs, to dwell in their midst. What joy the people must have felt! It is still the Lord's desire today that He dwell within us and be glorified, as our bodies are transformed into His temple by the new birth in Jesus Christ (John 14:23; 1 Cor. 6:19; Rev. 21:3) which gives the believer joy in their salvation. The Israelites were constantly reminded of their duty to honour, obey, glorify and worship God because of the tabernacle and the pillar of cloud by day and fire by night which signified His presence in their midst. By this pillar of His presence the Lord led His people through the wilderness until they came to Canaan, their long awaited destination.

The Lord has promised in His Word that while we, His children, are in the wilderness of this world, He will guide, direct and be in our midst through His Spirit and Son, our Lord Jesus (Matt. 18:20; Luke 1:79).

Prayer for today: *O Great God and Father, by faith we are in You and You in us. May the cloud of Your presence cover me and may Your glory fill me so that I will be all You intend me to be.*

Introduction to
The Book of Mark

Who was the author of this Gospel? Traditionally, he is seen as the young man whose mother's home was the central meeting place in Jerusalem for the early Christians (Acts 12:12). He was the same "John Mark" who travelled with Barnabas and Saul to Antioch (Acts 12:25), later leaving them at Perga (on the first missionary journey) and returning to Jerusalem (Acts 13:13). Twelve or thirteen years later, he was reconciled to Paul, proving "useful" in an assistant's role (Col.4:10; 2 Tim.4:11; Philemon 24). Most importantly (in terms of the genesis of this book), he was so closely associated with Peter that the apostle referred to him as "Mark, my son" (1 Peter 5:13).

Mark wasn't an apostle as such, but he was intimately knowledgeable about the life and works of Jesus — not just as a young boy looking on, but as a confidant of Peter and a participant in some of the missionary ministries of Paul.

The scholar, F.C.Grant, suggests that Mark's Gospel was written "backwards, from the passion story to the Baptism; for the passion story dominates the narrative almost from the outset" (*The Growth of the Gospels*, Abingdon Press 1933, pp.136-137). There's no question that the servant/martyr, Jesus, dominates this Gospel and lends credence to the common belief of scholars that Mark wrote not to Jews, but to the early Gentile Christians of the Roman empire. These were Christians who were already facing growing persecution and martyrdom for their refusal to worship the emperor/gods of Rome, insisting rather that Jesus of Nazareth was their Lord and King.

This is why many introductions to the Gospel of Mark will draw your attention to chapters 10:43-45 and 8:34-37 as key verses. Mark presents Jesus, not in kingly terms as did Matthew, but as suffering servant (like Isaiah). Jesus serves mankind even to the point of death. The implied question of Mark's Gospel is, "can we do anything less?"

Key Verse: Mark 1:15 *"The time is fulfilled, and the kingdom of God is at hand. Repent, and believe in the Gospel."*

After Mark tells us about John the Baptist and his ministry of repentance in preparing for the coming of Messiah, he immediately gets into the ministry of Jesus. Jesus' ministry is characterized by the message, "the kingdom of God is near, repent and believe the good news". (Repentance is fundamental in Jesus' ministry. It is seen in terms of turning around and walking away from one's sin.) We see Him calling the disciples in verses 14-20, then, as He gets to Capernaum, a fascinating incident occurs. An unclean spirit cries out and says, "What do you want with us, Jesus of Nazareth? Have You come to destroy us? I know who You are — the Holy One of God!"

Notice that the evil spirit knows Jesus' identity. In the spirit dimension it's no secret who Jesus is. If there is any secret at all, it's in the realm of men. Ironically, it's the evil spirit who makes a sort of confession of faith. This is not necessarily faith to believe, but at least faith to accept that Jesus is who He says He is. Jesus dealt with the evil spirit directly and cast it out. The people, predictably, were astonished. In their amazement, they saw Him as a teacher with a new teaching, with an authority that was absolutely remarkable. A little later on in the chapter, as Jesus was healing and delivering people from demon possession, he commands the demons not to speak, because they knew who He was. Tie this in with the several instances where Jesus tells people He has healed not to talk about their healing, and you see a fascinating picture of a Savior, Deliverer and Messiah who, on one hand is exposing His ministry in history, and even at the same time is trying somehow to hide it.

Perhaps one observation which can be made here relates to our desire to follow Jesus' example. We should be careful that we don't sensationalize the spiritual ministries of healing and deliverance. Jesus saw healing and deliverance as a private thing between the person and the Spirit of God. We certainly shouldn't attempt to make of this supernatural ministry more than Jesus Himself made of it.

Prayer for today: *We pray, oh Lord, that as we read the book of Mark, we will receive a fresh glimpse of Your example of servanthood that we can follow in loving our neighbours as ourselves.*

Key Verse: Mark 2:17 *"Those who are well have no need of a physician, but those who are sick. I did not come to call the righteous, but sinners, to repentance."*

In this chapter, Jesus really does and says some radical things. First of all, He heals a paralytic, which in itself is outstanding, but precedes the healing by saying to this fellow who has dropped in from the roof, "Son, your sins are forgiven". It's no wonder the teachers of the Law were upset. Nobody has the right to forgive sins but God alone, and I think we would all agree with their comment. But the fact is that Jesus was someone unlike anyone else in history. He then goes on from this outstanding event to say that the ones who qualify for this kind of salvation He is freely giving out are not the religious, nor the healthy, nor the righteous people, but those who are sick — the sinners.

This, of course, goes against the grain of current religious thought. The idea, then as now, in the rabbinic tradition, was that a man obtained righteousness through good works. But Jesus contradicts tradition and says the ones who are really diseased are those qualifying for salvation. Then He takes some shots at two aspects of piety that spring out of the current view of righteousness. He first of all says that fasting is not necessarily a factor in pleasing God. He, in effect, was saying, "Look, I represent a whole new age, a new kingdom, a new message". And in that context new wineskins are necessary for new wine. There's a whole new horizon to be explored. The same applies to Sabbath observance, a very important and holy aspect of Jewish life. But Jesus, seeing the Sabbath becoming a bondage, says the Sabbath was made for man not man for the Sabbath. In other words, if the Sabbath does not benefit us, there's no way we are going to benefit it. So He focuses in again on God's commitment to the healthiness, or holiness, of man and his need for rest and recreation. Jesus is a Healer who saves, a Savior who heals, and a Free Spirit of the highest order.

Prayer for today: *Thank You, Lord, that You have the right to forgive sins which You exercised with the paralytic in this reading, even before You healed him. May we be like the four men and bring our loved ones to you, Lord Jesus.*

Read Mark 3 · March 26

Key Verse: Mark 3:27 *"Stretch out your hand..."*

Two things stand out in this chapter. First of all, Jesus heals someone who has had a withered hand all his life. Notice that Jesus asks a man who has never used his hand before to stretch it out. This seems to be a rather unreasonable demand. The man probably expected Jesus to take the initiative in this healing; instead, He looks at the man and says, "You take the initiative. You stretch out your hand." So he did. As he made the attempt, Jesus empowered him.

This is a good word to us. When we seek God's touch in our lives we should, from time to time, think in terms of touching Him. We should take the initiative. The other thing standing out in this chapter is the mention of the "unpardonable sin". (Once again there is a record of evil spirits expressing belief that Jesus is the Son of God.) The religious teachers explain Jesus' power to deliver from demonic possession as demonic power itself. In fact, they go so far as to say that He is Himself possessed by Beelzebub, the "ruler of demons". To this Jesus says a house divided against itself cannot stand, and then He goes on to talk about the unpardonable sin — the sin against the Holy Spirit. Many people, feeling spiritually depressed, or just spiritually flat, often think they have committed the unpardonable sin. But look at the context. Jesus is speaking to religious leaders who should know better, but are in fact attributing the power of the Holy Spirit to Satan. He says it is absolutely unacceptable to credit Satan with what is the work of God. As long as one persists willfully in that kind of spiritual blindness and unbelief, he is beyond the reach of Grace.

The unpardonable sin is a deliberate, willful act of unbelief, where one maliciously impugns the work of the Spirit of God. I've been in the ministry twenty years and I have yet to see anyone guilty of this sin. And I probably never will.

Prayer for today: *Lord, May we learn about active faith from the account of the healing of the withered hand. Your Word tells us that the man had to take the first step, stretching out his hand, before the miracle came, help us to put our faith into action before the answer comes.*

Read Mark 4 *March 27*

Key Verse: Mark 4:9 *"He who has ears to hear, let him hear!"*

This has been called by some commentators the chapter of parables. Mark suggests in verses 2, 33 & 34, that the parables here are just some of the many Jesus taught. Two of them deal with the kingdom and what the kingdom of heaven is like; the other two talk about a proper response to the gospel. Just a few comments about that first parable, that of the sower. It is not so much about seed or sowers, as it is about soil. Broadcasting or scattering seed was often used as an illustration of the act of teaching, and the students were seen as the soil. Some students produced a harvest and others produced nothing — only barrenness.

The point of the parable is that any broadcasting or sowing of the truth involves some loss. And I don't think we can assume from this that because there were four kinds of soil, and only one kind bore fruit, that we should expect a return of only twenty-five percent. I feel we can assume that the good ground is most of the field. Nevertheless, men can choose to hear or not to hear. They can also choose to respond or not to respond. So it's not a case of passively bearing fruit, or passively deflecting the seed. Rather, it's a matter of one actively allowing the seed to take root in one's heart. Notice the conclusion of the chapter. It's the story of Jesus calming the storm. I think the outstanding aspect of this is the terror and consternation in the minds of the disciples as they ask, "Who is this Jesus anyway? Even the winds and the waves obey Him." Obviously the disciples hadn't tuned in to know what the demons already knew. We've seen in Mark that evil spirits were very much convinced of who Jesus was. It's ironic that Jesus should have to take three years to demonstrate who He was to an increasingly recalcitrant and hard-headed group of disciples. Perhaps we shouldn't be too hard on the religious leaders who misunderstood and rejected Jesus. His own disciples, our spiritual forefathers, not only misunderstood Him, they even forsook Him during the critical hours of His passion.

If the evil spirits recognize Jesus only because they dwell in the darker regions of the spirit realm, we shouldn't be surprised that the disciples didn't recognize Him until He had been resurrected in the space and time realm. Later, as their hearts were quickened by the Day of Pentecost events, the disciples became powerful witnesses to who Jesus really was — the eternal Son of God.

Prayer for today: *All praise is due You, oh God, for the storms You calm in our lives. Grant that we might have the peace in the midst of the storm You demonstrated by sleeping in the bottom of the boat.*

Read Mark 5 *March 28*

Key Verse: Mark 5:34 "*...your faith has made you well. Go in peace, and be healed..."*

Here we have the stories of a dead girl and a sick woman. The woman had an affliction which had disabled her for twelve years. What's more, it brought with it a ceremonial uncleanness — which meant she was a bit of an outcast. Because of this, she lived with a deep sense of shame, affecting her self-esteem and self-confidence to the point where she would shrink from coming to Jesus openly and of easily confessing afterwards that she'd touched Him. The dead girl, on the other hand, had been alive as long as the woman had been sick. Her father, Jairus, had come boldly to Jesus, and it was while on His way to Jarius' house that the timid woman had reached out to touch Him. And so the two stories converge.

Jairus had encountered a sudden sorrow after twelve years of joy. The woman had been living with twelve years of deferred hope, longing for the day her affliction would cease, but finding every new day was just as bad as the last. It could very well be that she had spent most of her money on doctors and medicine, even while the young girl had been merrily skipping through a carefree childhood. Enter Jesus, the compassionate and versatile healer.

To the woman who had been sick for twelve years, He says, "Your faith has healed you, take heart." As for the girl, He goes to her house where a noisy crowd has already begun singing death dirges. He tells them to stop because the girl "is not dead but asleep". Here is an instance where Jesus faced open mockery. Nevertheless, He went inside the house, took the girl by the hand, ordered her to get up, and she got up. Jesus had done it again. In one case, twelve years of hope, suddenly dashed, had been given new life. In the other case, twelve years of sorrow with no hope of release, had suddenly ended and a whole new life begun. On the one hand, a timid touch by the sick one, on the other, a commanding touch by the Healer, both resulted in the kingdom of heaven coming amongst mankind once again. All because of faith in Jesus.

Prayer for today: *Thank You, dear Lord, for being the Great Physician with whom nothing is impossible. We pray today for Your divine touch in our bodies, that we may be enabled to serve You with all our strength.*

Read Mark 6 *March 29*

Key Verse: Mark 5:50 *"Be of good cheer! It is I; do not be afraid."*

If there's anything for which Jesus is most remembered by the secular world (apart from the Christmas story), it's something recorded in this chapter: Jesus walking on the water. He and the disciples had just finished a very labour-intensive (to say nothing of people-intensive) task, the feeding of the five thousand. He insisted His disciples take a break, in fact we read, "He made His disciples get into the boat..." while He, himself, went "to the mountain to pray." Later in the night, He saw His disciples straining at the oars as they fought the wind. So He walked out to them...on the water!

The disciples, predictably, were terrified. They were sure a ghost was walking on the waves, and cried out in fear. Jesus responded with the most comforting words in all of scripture, "Be of good cheer! It is I; do not be afraid." The key words are, "It is I". It's Jesus, and if it's He, then everything is okay. "Take heart. It is I."

Someone has rightly said that the only adequate faith for deep distress is a person. Central in this vast created order is a person — *the* Person, the God of Love. Underneath all human sorrow and fear are the everlasting arms of a God who "so loved the world". John MacMurray has wisely said,

> "The sense that the world as a whole is personal is the very heart of religious experience. To the man with the sense of God alive in his soul the world is neither a mechanical system, nor an evolving something. It is something made by Someone, and brought to life by Someone, controlled, indwelt, loved by an infinite person, who is its meaning, its reality, and its good."
> *(The Christian World)*

Those three words, "It is I", are pivotal to faith. We cry out in our distress, "O God!", and we hear in reply, "It is I". When we hear those words, any storm is suddenly put in perspective. A peace "that passes understanding" calms the waves and we rest.

Prayer for today: *Lord, we're grateful today for the way You come to meet us in a personal and loving way when we cry out for You; what peace You bring!*

Read Mark 7   March 30

Key Verse: Mark 7:8 "... *Laying aside the commandment of God, you hold the tradition of men...*"

If ever you're tempted to reduce God's work in your life to a system or formula, read this chapter. In the first half we read about Jesus' revulsion for human systems and traditions. Specifically, He attacks formulas for righteousness. The issue was what is, and what isn't, "kosher" (or "clean"). The Pharisees were upset because Jesus' disciples were eating food without washing their hands beforehand.

Jesus reacts by quoting Isaiah 29:13, where the Lord speaks out against external lip service and the teachings of men. Then He knocks the tradition of neglecting one's parent's financial needs by designating their rightful portion "corban" (a gift devoted to God). And then He offends religious tradition even more by saying that what we eat or drink has nothing to do with defilement. Rather it's the internals of man that defile him. Uncleanness is not an "outside" issue at all — it's an "inside" one. So chuck the man-made rules. God looks where no other person can look: on the heart. Then, just in case you think you can get Jesus to do what you want if you're clever enough to discover His healing and miracle-working formula, read on.

In the latter half of the chapter, we see Jesus healing a woman's demon-possessed daughter, not with a touch, or a command, but by a semitic riddle-like interchange, a clever answer and a quiet word. Then while you're still trying to figure that one out, He goes on to heal a deaf and partially dumb man by doing seven things: He (1) takes the man aside. (2) touches the man's tongue. (3) spits. (4) touches the man's tongue. (5) looks up to heaven. (6) sighs and (7) shouts, "Be opened!".

So where's the system? The formula? There is none. Ultimately we're all subject to God's sovereignty. He won't be labelled, figured out, or put in a box. Which, among other things, makes prayer quite an adventure!

Prayer for today: *We pray today, oh God, that we will never be guilty of trying to manipulate Your divine workings in our life by using a formula or system. We know You are sovereign.*

Read Mark 8   *March 31*

Key Verse: Mark 8:18 *"Having eyes, do you not see? And having ears, do you not hear? And do you not remember?"*

This chapter gives us a fascinating insight into the frailty of human nature. Beginning in verse 14 we have a story of the disciples forgetting to bring bread on a boat trip. All they had was one loaf, and they were obviously concerned. Jesus saw their concern and made the most unusual comment. He says, "Beware of the leaven (yeast) of the Pharisees and the leaven of Herod." The disciples were somewhat flumoxed by this and tried to figure out why Jesus was scolding them. They thought it might be because they'd failed to plan ahead. But that wasn't the problem. The problem was that they had forgotten how Jesus had miraculously provided bread for them, and thousands of others, before. He looks at them and asks if their hearts have become hardened, or their eyes blind, or their ears deaf. "Don't you remember?" Jesus asks. Or better yet, "Don't you see?" Then He recalls the feeding of the five thousand and recounts the baskets of bread left over.

It's in this context that the word "yeast" comes into play. The yeast of the Scribes, the Pharisees, and Herod had something to do with a secular mind set. The natural or carnal way of looking at things can effectively block Christ's provision. Jesus' yeast not only makes bread rise, it multiplies bread! He then reemphasizes the point by reminding them of the feeding of the four thousand; but the disciples don't get the point. The fact is that Jesus can supply the need. His track record proves it. And to be able to trust Him in a simple way for one's daily bread is perhaps the bottom line, the litmus test, to being His disciple. This isn't to suggest that we do away with the means He has provided us in terms of daily work and wages to supply a need. Nevertheless, even in that we must recognize that any good thing we have has come from God.

Prayer for today: *Lord, You are Jehovah Jireh, our provider. Help us to rest assured in Your provision, remembering how you've provided for us in the past. May we look, with the eye of faith, beyond our natural circumstances.*

Proclaiming the Good News of Jesus

— Since 1962 —

THE CROSSROADS CHRISTIAN COMMUNICATIONS FAMILY OF MINISTRIES:

100 HUNTLEY STREET: Daily Christian television since 1977. Viewers obtain counselling and prayer through dozens of telephone counselling centres.

CIRCLE SQUARE: Top quality Christian programming for children. This fast-paced weekly show is popular in many countries around the world.

CIRCLE SQUARE RANCHES: Started as a follow-up to the Circle Square program, there are now nine ranches offering summer camping programs for children and year-round retreats.

CMP: Christian Missions Productions has produced Christian programs in 17 languages other than English.

NITE LITE: Late night live open-line television in which the host matches real problems of callers with the answers of the Gospel.

HEART TO HEART FAMILY MINISTRIES: Marriage and family counselling and seminars promoting Biblical wholeness in the home.

KINGDOM ADVENTURE: State-of-the-art children's programming combining puppetry and animation to teach Biblical truths and values.

CHRISTIAN BROADCAST ACADEMY: Television production training for men and women of vision who want this medium used for the Gospel.

DAVID MAINSE CRUSADES: Interdenominational, area-wide evangelistic crusades.

E.R.D.F.: The Emergency Response and Development Fund: For years, TV viewers have responded whenever stories of human need have been featured.

If you would like information on becoming a partner with us through your prayerful and financial support, please write your request to: C.C.C.I., 100 Huntley Street, Toronto, Ontario, Canada M4Y 2L1.